~and then there were Four

BERLIN MEMORIES—1930s and BEYOND

Ellen Stein   **Marcelle Robinson**

Daisy Roessler   **Lisa Klein**

Library of Congress Control Number: 2005907080
ISBN: Hardcover   1-59926-336-X
                             Softcover   1-59926-335-1

This book was printed in the United States of America.

To order additional copies of this book, contact:
Xlibris Corporation
1-888-795-4274
www.Xlibris.com
Orders@Xlibris.com
26774

~and then there were Four

A tradition in 1930s Germany—and still practiced today—was to give each new student on the first day of school a large, elaborately decorated cardboard cone, called a "SCHULTUETE", filled with chocolates, marzipan, other candy and fruit.

These photos of Marcelle, Ellen, Daisy and Lisa were taken on the first day each girl entered First Grade in Berlin.

COVER DESIGN by Ellen Rozanski Stein

TABLE OF CONTENTS

Ellen Stein

Ellen Rozanski Stein

Ellen Rozanski Stein has lived in the United States since 1948. She is proud to have become a citizen and is still amazed and grateful that she feels so at home here.

It has been a long road from her childhood in Berlin, Germany, that included a nine-year stop-over in England during and after World War II, to her arrival in the U.S. She finally has a sense of belonging to a place and a country.

She is now retired after a career as a Fashion Designer during which she created both wedding gowns and lingerie. In addition, Ellen's life-long interest in sculpture developed into a second career of making Biblical Figures out of antique textiles. These have been exhibited and sold at the Jewish Museum in New York City.

Ellen recently celebrated her long postponed Bat Mitzvah and is pleased to have completed a year of serious studies for this event. She resides in Westchester County, New York.

ELLEN STEIN - CONTENTS

Prologue

I was born in Berlin, Germany in 1926. My parents—Ryvkah Koslow and Aron Rozanski had decided at an early age not to remain in Bialystok, the large Polish city where they were both born. For several generations both their families had been residents of this city when it was still a part of Russia. My mother Ryvkah's family was of strong Zionist orientation. Most of them finally emigrated to Palestine.

My father Aron's family were Orthodox Jews—my grandmother Malkah wore a ritual wig—and they observed all the laws a Jewish family was obligated to do. My paternal grandfather Nissan Rozanski was a contractor and skilled sign painter. My grandmother was a proper Jewish housewife who raised seven children during the difficult years of the German occupation of Poland in the tumultuous years of World War I.

The family of my mother Ryvkah was much more assimilated. My maternal grandfather Simcha Koslow and my grandmother Elkah believed in a secular education for their six children. Grandfather was a cabinet maker who designed and manufactured furniture much in demand in their city—and my enterprising grandmother owned and operated a Children's Wear Store. This necessitated frequent buying trips to wholesalers in Warsaw for her and her oldest daughter Ryvkah, who later became my mother. They were also ardent Zionists and, after my grandmother's death, grandfather decided to emigrate to Palestine with his children.

His two oldest children, my mother and her brother Grisha, objected to this. They did not want to be pioneers in that far-off land of Palestine. Instead, the bright lights of Berlin beckoned. They decided to join my father-to-be Aron who had also thought that Bialystok held no future for him. He had paid a Polish potato farmer to hide him under a wagon load of potato sacks, and illegally smuggled himself over the border into Germany.

My father and my uncle rented an apartment together in Berlin, and because my mother came to stay with them to "keep house"the inevitable happened. Aron and Ryvkah fell very much in love. In due course there was a marriage, and I was born. I have vague memories of our first home, an apartment on Oranienburger Strasse, which we soon left for a modern apartment in the suburb of Reinickendorf. Then—a big step up socially—to apartments, first on Marburger Strasse, and later Niebuhr Strasse in the elegant and fashionable sector of Charlottenburg. Niebuhr Strasse was close to my favorite destination when shopping with my mother. This was the famous KaDeWe Department Store.

My childhood could have been, and should have been, tranquil and secure. My father had a successful contracting business—employing about fifteen men—and my mother was active in volunteer work at our local synagogue.

But when I was seven years old, the Nazis made their appearance. This resulted in the tainting of my childhood memories. I acquired the feelings of inferiority—and constant fear—that the Nazis quickly tried to instill in every Jewish resident of Berlin and Germany.

My daily routine of attending school, and playing with my friends, was suddenly an obstacle course that little girls should not have had to experience. I remember watching my parents fail time after time in their frantic efforts to obtain visas for us to emigrate to any country that would permit us entry.

Fortunately our amazing escape aboard a British fishing trawler brought us to freedom in England and to safety from the Nazis. But we were still not entirely safe. For years the Luftwaffe bombed Britain during World War II. However, this time we were not being persecuted and singled out for being Jewish. We were in a war that affected the entire country of Great Britain.

Finally, after much wandering and many life changes, here I am, recalling—together with my school friends Daisy, Lisa and Marcelle—some of the adventures we shared as children, the dangers we somehow avoided, and the miracle that we are, even now, connected by our enduring friendship and our shared memories.

Chapter One

Berlin 1933
The Beginning

The first Nazi I ever saw rode past us on a bicycle. I was seven years old, playing Hopscotch with my little sister Silvia on the sidewalk in front of our apartment building at 12, Marburgerstrasse in Berlin. We lived next door to the post office, so when I saw the young man park his bicycle and walk into the building, I assumed he was a mailman. He wore a uniform I'd never seen before. It was tan, with a red, white, and black armband that had a hooked cross on it.

That evening at supper I told my parents about the mailman in his strange new uniform. My parents glanced at each other, and my mother said, "That was no mailman. That was a Nazi." I wanted to know what a Nazi was. Papa, in no uncertain terms, told me never to go near a Nazi, and never to stare at any of them.

My parents, Ryvkah and Aron Rozanski, had arrived in Berlin in 1924, from Bialystok, Poland, hoping to find a safe, secure home away from the anti-Semitism and pogroms they had grown up with in their homeland. They married in Berlin, and Silvia and I were born there.

Now we were facing a new threat. The Nazis appeared in ever greater numbers on the streets, and we started to hear Hitler's rants about Jews on the radio and in the newsreels that were shown at the cinema.

Soon after that, all Jewish school children in Berlin were expelled from the public schools. Our presence apparently was considered defiling to our Aryan fellow students. Just before that event, I remember how hurt I was when I arrived in my classroom one morning. I went to my regular school desk that I shared with my best friend Gisela. She gathered her skirt about her knees and moved as far away from me as she could without falling off the seat. I asked her what was the matter. She said that her two brothers had joined the Hitler Youth and had told her to stay away from Jews because they were unclean and evil. I still remember the hurt feeling—that for the first time in my life I was being rejected for a totally unfair reason. I never saw Gisela again because, when I arrived home in tears, Mutti and Papa decided to find a Jewish school for me.

Gisela's rejection of me happened at the same time as the Nazi edict about Jewish children in public schools. So it was right for me to be enrolled in the Jewish school of the Synagogue Fasanen Strasse. From there I graduated to the Lyceum of the school Addass Yisroel in Siegmunds Hof. At least in school I was safe from the intolerable anti-Semitism that was spreading like a virus over Berlin. Of course this did not prevent us from having to run the gauntlet of Hitler Youths when they congregated at the doors of Jewish schools to jeer at us arriving for classes.

One boy was more creative than his friends. He found a stick, dipped it in dog excrement, then started chasing us while waving this weapon and threatening to wipe it clean on the clothes of us "Kleine Judenschweine" (Little Jew pigs). When our school was forcibly closed, following Kristallnacht, most Jewish school children had to travel long distances to attend the one Jewish school that remained open in Berlin on Wilsnackerstrasse. I attended it until our escape to England.

Chapter Two

Berlin 1933 (and on)
The Little Blue Pushke

On the kitchen wall in our Berlin apartment there always hung a little blue and white tin box my parents called "the Pushke". It was a bright blue, cube-shaped tin, with white Hebrew letters on the front that spelled Keren Kayemet Leyisroel, and there was a white Star of David below the printing. On top was a slot for the deposit of coins. Papa told us that the money we saved in this bank would be used to help buy land in Palestine, so Jews all over the world would have a homeland some day.

Growing up in the stressful anti-Semitic environment of Nazi Berlin, I absolutely could not imagine such a country ever existing in the future. A place where all Jews could go? A country that would just allow us to come in and live there? A safe place to which we could escape without having Affidavits and Visas, or worrying about high Quota numbers? This seemed as impossible to me as the "Schlaraffen-Land" that existed in German fairy tales where all wishes came true.

Every week, when Silvia and I received our allowance from Papa, he walked us over to the Pushke and supervised our sometimes not so voluntary donations for a Jewish homeland. Every time the Pushke was filled, Mutti took it to the office at our Temple in Fasanenstrasse where we were members.

This Pushke traveled in our hand luggage to Hamburg, to Grimsby and then London. It was immediately affixed by Papa to the kitchen wall of our apartment in Kilburn. No matter how little we had, the land in Palestine HAD to be purchased, and the Pushke had to be filled. It stayed with us through the Blitzkrieg and the bombings. It remained a part of my parents' lives even after they arrived in America in 1950. Papa again hung it on their kitchen wall in their apartment in Manhattan and there it remained.

Israel had now become a State but my parents continued to make regular purchases of Israel Bonds by saving for them in that battered Pushke hanging on the kitchen wall. When my son Steven was born, the Israel bonds my parents purchased as gifts for him were paid for with money accumulated in that little blue and white box. Now, instead of Pfennigs and Marks, instead of Shillings and Pounds, the deposits to the Pushke were in Quarters and Dollars.

The Pushke stayed on the wall after my father died. My mother maintained the tradition of the little blue box by saving for Israel bonds that she continued to give as family gifts till she died as she had wished, peacefully in her own home in 1980.

The Pushke tradition is one of the happy memories of my childhood in Berlin, my teen years in London, and finally of my parents' lives in the United States.

Chapter Three

Berlin in the 1930s
Shabbes

I used to look forward to the summer holidays when school was closed. On Friday mornings, Silvia and I got to go shopping with Mutti for the ingredients for our Shabbes Dinner. Early in the morning, Mutti prepared for the shopping trip. Our bathtub was filled with cold water, for the live fish that we were going to bring home, flapping and wriggling in the wet newspaper it was wrapped in. Silvia really enjoyed carrying the string shopping bag with this live cargo. I found it very upsetting. But Mutti said that this was the only way to have really fresh gefilte fish.

After the stop at the fishmongers, where Mutti checked out the fish swimming in the large glass tank, and picked the unfortunate victim, our next stop was the kosher butcher, for a chicken that would be made into Mutti's delicious soup. The chicken with feathers intact was carefully selected. It had to be a mature hen so there would be the unlaid eggs inside that Silvia and I absolutely loved to eat.

Once Mutti had selected the chicken, it was taken to the back room of the butcher shop, where the "Chicken Plucker", usually a very old woman, sat. Watching her hands deftly pull all the feathers out was pure theater for Silvia and me. She then held the naked carcass over a Bunsen burner, to scorch the pinfeathers that were left in the pale skin. The smell was sharp and pungent. Both Silvia and I couldn't wait for this magic moment. We loved that acrid smell.

The next stop was the greengrocer, where Mutti carefully selected the "soup-greens" that would be boiled with the chicken to add their flavor to the broth. As soon as we got home, Silvia ran to the tub of cold water, to release the gasping, flapping fish, and then stood in wonder as it started swimming in circles in our bathtub.

Meanwhile, the preparations for the evening meal began. First the Challah dough had to be mixed and put in a large bowl, covered with a special cloth, so it could rise and then be punched down by Mutti. It never ceased to amaze us that out of this sticky mess would come the fragrant Challah over which Mutti said a blessing at the evening meal.

The chicken was cut up with special shears used only for that purpose. The unborn eggs were carefully removed and very gently lowered into the boiling soup pot. Next the fish was brought into the kitchen. And this is when I ran to my room and covered my ears. I always expected the fish to scream as it was deftly beheaded by Mutti. Silvia watched intently. She enjoyed this execution and looked forward to it all week.

The fish needed much preparation—grinding, chopping, seasoning and mixing. This mixture was formed into patties and poached in a fragrant liquid that Mutti had already prepared. Then came the rolling and braiding of the Challah. I loved to help Mutti make the elegantly shaped loaves that were brushed with beaten egg yolk. To do this Mutti used a large feather brought home from the Chicken Plucker.

These loaves were then put into the oven from which soon wafted the most heavenly, yeasty odors. When all the food had been prepared—cooked, baked, fried and poached—we helped Mutti get the dining table ready for the Sabbath. She brought out one of her snowy white damask tablecloths—(the green and peach one with the matching napkins was reserved for Passover)—and the polished three-armed candelabrum, into which I was allowed to insert three white candles.

Our "good" plates were set on the table as well as our silver tableware, all polished and gleaming. When everything was ready, and with the apartment filled with the wonderful aroma of freshly baked Challah and gefilte fish, we gathered around the table. Mutti stood in front of the candles, her hair covered with a scarf, while Papa stood next to her. She lit the candles and covered her eyes with her hands, quietly saying the prayer welcoming the Sabbath.

Papa then put one hand on Silvia's head and his other hand on mine, and also said a prayer. He blessed the wine and, from his silver cup, we all got a sip. Mutti said the blessing over the Challah, which was covered with an embroidered cloth, and cut the slices for us to eat.

Silvia and I helped bring the food in from the kitchen, which was connected by a long corridor to the dining room. The soup, with matzo-balls, homemade noodles and the tiny unborn eggs, came first, then the gefilte fish and the very tender boiled chicken pieces with salad. Some homemade cake, usually baked with fresh fruit on top, finished the meal.

Papa and Mutti remained at the table with us, telling stories of their childhood in Bialystok. This was always my favorite time of the week. I felt so secure in our rituals, our beautiful Sabbath prayers, my mother blessing the candles, and Papa blessing us. This was never repeated in England or America, except during the Jewish Holidays.

Chapter Four

Berlin, Early 1930s
Family Times

My father was a contractor and, until forced to close his business, was able to afford his family a middle class lifestyle. On Sundays my parents wanted to get us into the fresh air of the country. Just getting away from Berlin's ever present Swastika banners hanging from buildings, and the Nazis goose-stepping down major avenues, was a relief.

My father bought a small Fiat car for these trips and Silvia and I looked forward to those drives into the countryside. My mother always prepared a picnic lunch because we were never sure if we'd find a restaurant that served Jewish customers. My father took his camera. I still cherish the photos he took using a time delay so he could include himself in the pictures by clicking, and then running to join us in the family group.

My mother was determined that Silvia and I would learn to swim even though my parents were terrible swimmers. So we often drove to a resort area outside Berlin called Wannsee, and were given swimming lessons in the lake. I hated this especially because we were suspended from what I can best describe as a fishing pole attached by a rope to our waist. Then an instructor shouted orders to us on how to move our arms and legs. To this day, all I can do is splash in the water. I never learned to swim although my fearless little sister became quite good at it.

Saturday mornings was "Shirley Temple" time at the local movie theater. Silvia and I were sent off to enjoy this wholesome entertainment, with Shirley speaking and singing in German. My sister proudly told everyone that the girl supplying the lip-synched German voice for Shirley was a schoolmate of hers.

My parents' marriage was a real love match. They were married for more than 50 years. During their lives, they emigrated three times: first from eastern Europe into Germany, then our escape from Germany to England, and finally from England to the United States where they both proudly became citizens, as did Silvia and I.

Chapter Five

Berlin 1933
Grandpa from Palestine

Mutti's father, Simcha Kozlov, lived in Haifa, Palestine. He had emigrated from Bialystok with four of his children, Abraham, (Zundel) Yacov, (Yankel) Meyer, and Shoshana (Shanne) after my Oma Elkah died in the early 1920s and whom, of course, I never knew.

In the 1930s my Opa Simcha in Haifa decided to remarry, and came to Berlin on a visit to look for a suitable bride. He stayed with us, in our apartment on Marburger Strasse, next to the post office. I, as his oldest grandchild, was in my glory. It was the first time we had met. I had been named after his late, much loved wife Elkah, and he and I formed an instant bond. He was a very distinguished looking man, tall, with gray hair and a neatly trimmed little beard, and always elegantly dressed.

He had found a good existence in Palestine as a cabinet-maker designing and crafting really excellent furniture, which was still in use when I visited Israel more than fifty years later. He spoke both Yiddish and German so we were able to communicate easily. Every day we were off on long walks. I especially loved visits to the Berlin Zoo with ice cream as a daily treat. Opa Simcha's stay with us was a totally wonderful experience for me. After Silvia's birth, my parents' attention had been divided, but to my Opa, I was the most important child in the world.

I was later told that when Opa had received Papa's telegram from Berlin telling him of my birth, he went to the grave of Rachel, the Biblical Matriarch. This monument is situated at the outskirts of Jerusalem and, following an ancient tradition, he measured out a length of red ribbon by circling the grave on foot. He rolled up this ribbon, tied it and mailed it to Berlin as a good-luck talisman for me, his first grandchild. My parents gave this ribbon to me when Silvia and I left London for Braunston just as the war was about to begin. I still have it and carry it in my purse always.

Of course I didn't know that the reason for his visit was to find a nice German-Jewish single woman who would be willing to marry him and return with him to his home in Haifa. He did, indeed, find such a person. We all liked Tante Lotte. Gentle and very friendly, she was a rather large woman always trussed up in heavy shapeless corsets. I never saw her clothed in anything but black satin dresses. After two months, Opa and Tante Lotte were married in Berlin, and returned to Haifa together. When I visited Israel in 1984, I was shown a family photo album and noticed a snapshot of a laughing, tanned, woman with tousled hair, dressed in an open-necked white blouse. I asked my cousins who she was and was told that this was Tante Lotte ! I could hardly believe it. When she left us in Berlin, she was a serious, straight-laced woman, always in heavy black dresses, with her hair in marcelled waves plastered to her head. Now I was looking at the image of a radiant, casually dressed woman, with her hair tumbling into her eyes. No one had to tell me that she and Opa had been very happy together.

While we were still in Berlin, we often visited Tante Lotte's elderly mother who lived in a nursing home. She was wheelchair bound and much too frail to accompany her daughter to Palestine. How I admired this elderly woman, whom we addressed as "Muttel"—little mother—for not standing in the way of her spinster daughter's chance at happiness. She sent her off to a faraway land with her blessings knowing that she probably would never see her daughter again.

Mutti told me this when we drove to visit her once a month, which we did regularly till we left Berlin in such a hurry. I hope she died a peaceful death before the issue of the Nazi edict to kill all superfluous elderly Jews in hospitals and nursing homes.

Chapter Six

Berlin 1935
Street Singers

We were still living in Marburger Strasse. I remember
the windows of our apartment facing the trees and flowers
in the courtyard, so I must have been nine years old. Street
singers came into the courtyard every day and sang sad songs
about being rejected by their mother and not knowing who
their father was. I didn't understand this at all. How could
you not know who your father was?

These singers wandered the streets and courtyards of
Berlin, singing for the coins that were thrown, wrapped in
bits of newspaper, from the windows, One day they stopped
coming into our courtyard. I missed their plaintive songs
and asked Mutti what had happened to the singing beggars.

She told me that the Nazi-controlled city government had
prohibited both the street entertainers from singing and the
street artists from drawing big roses in colored chalk on the
sidewalk. I used to stand, in absolute amazement, while a very
poorly dressed man brushed off the sidewalk in front of our

apartment building with a long-handled broom, then opened a box of vividly colored chalks, and started drawing roses on the rough pavement. These beautiful flowers were about a meter across, and to my uncritical eyes they were pure ART. The artist even had cleverly incorporated dew drops on the rose petals.

Appreciative passersby tossed coins onto these gorgeous flower pictures. After an hour or so, when the artist figured he'd gotten as many donations as he could in this location, he'd erase the chalk flowers with a cloth and move on to the next block. Then new laws came into effect, and Mutti told me that the singers and the artists would not come back ever again.

I really missed them. They were great entertainment and, I thought, very talented. Other street artists who disappeared at the same time were the men who had barrel organs and cute little monkeys. Each organ was on a wheeled cart, brightly painted with scenes depicting Italy. A protruding handle that the organist laboriously turned created the music. Some of these men also sang; Italian folk songs, Mutti said. The little monkey was dressed in a red suit, like a hotel bellboy in the movies we saw on Saturdays. I felt sad for the monkey because he was chained to the barrel organ with a long clanking chain, attached to a leather collar around his neck. He held a little bucket in which to collect coins from passersby.

Another regular street entertainer was the man who set up a table and put little tin dogs and dolls on display. He wound up each toy with a key causing them to start moving. The dogs wagged their tails, while the dolls played miniature violins, each moving her right arm up and down and holding a bow in her hand. With the dogs wound up, one could hear barking sounds, and the wound-up dolls played their violins to whistling music.

It didn't take me long to figure out that the man was making the sounds himself. He bent his head low, so adults could not see his lips move, but I was small, very observant, and saw his deception right away. I ran home to tell Mutti about my discovery, and was sure she would see to it that he would be prevented from cheating potential customers.

Mutti sat down and asked me to listen carefully to what she was about to say. She told me that men like this one were terribly poor, often elderly veterans of the"Great War" who could not find jobs. The sales they made in the street were their only income, and I was to stop staring at them and embarrassing them. She must have told Papa because a few days later he gave me money to buy one of the little dogs with the wagging tail. This toy was very flimsy and soon fell apart, but I had listened to Mutti and did not complain.

Chapter Seven

Berlin 1936
Journeys with Papa

I was ten years old when Papa decided I should meet his family in Bialystok. This would be my second trip to Poland, though I did not remember my first visit there at age four. That time both my parents traveled and brought eighteen-month-old Silvia as well as me. I knew I would meet all the people Papa had told me about: his father—my Opa (Grandpa) Nissan Rozanski; Papa's brothers, my Onkels Simcha and Zalmen, and his four sisters, my Tanten Taybe, Rochel, Peschka and Shayndel. I would also meet my cousin Melechke, Aunt Peshka's son who was only a year younger than I.

The train ride from Berlin to Poland turned out to be more exciting than I had expected. Papa had the habit of getting off at every stop and walking up and down the platform while the train was in the station. He liked to buy local brands of cigarettes for himself and candy for me, then hop back onto the train just as it started to move.

At the last station stop in Germany before the border crossing into Poland, the train began to move. Papa was nowhere in sight. I was paralyzed with fear. Here I was alone, approaching the Polish border. Papa had our visas and my passport in his pocket. I envisioned being arrested by the German border guards and put in jail. As I took a deep breath and started to sob hysterically, the compartment door opened and a very contrite Papa rushed in. He apologized, saying he had been buying chocolate for me and almost missed the train. This was not a good start for our trip.

The border crossing was not at all scary, and by the time we reached Bialystok I was happy to receive the very warm greetings of my aunts and uncles. They all had come to the main station in Bialystok to meet us. I loved riding in the horse-drawn carriage called a Droshky, so different from the taxis in Berlin or Papa's car.

We stayed at the apartment of my Uncle Simcha and his wife Anya. Every morning, for my breakfast Tante Anya—a slender, attractive woman with long black hair twisted in a braid—prepared a steaming bowl of Kasha (cooked buckwheat groats), with a large piece of fresh butter melting on top. Breakfast over, the visiting began. We visited all my aunts—vibrant and beautiful young women, with big smiles and sparkling eyes. All were accomplished at sewing and were very fashionably dressed.

On the second day, Papa took me to meet his father, my Opa. I was not prepared to meet this very sick old man. Even Papa had not known how seriously ill his father was. When I walked into Opa's room, he raised his arms, embraced me, and kissed both my hands. He had tears in his eyes—those same green eyes I see every day in my sister. But Opa was unable to speak. He sat in his chair and trembled constantly. Papa stood nearby translating my words to his father because my Yiddish was not very fluent and Opa did not speak German. Even though I was only ten years old, I realized that Opa and I would never meet again. And so it was; he died the year after our visit.

In the commercial center of Bialystok, Papa took me to a huge outdoor market where I saw things for sale that I had never seen before. There were candy stalls with swags of vividly colored marshmallow people covered with powdered sugar that were sold by the meter. Another stand exhibited large jars of conserved fruits and a big blue glass seltzer siphon. The customer chose a flavor of fruit from the display and, with a spoon that had a long handle, the vendor scooped a portion into a glass and filled it with cold seltzer, stirring all the while. This produced a delicious, fruity, sweet drink. It tasted better than any lemonade I had ever drunk in Berlin.

My aunts constantly fussed over me, hugging and kissing me, and telling me I was beautiful. I soaked up this attention with real delight. When it was time to leave, I reluctantly said goodbye to my aunts, to my uncle, and in a tearful last visit, to Opa Nissan.

We stayed in Warsaw for a few days before returning to Berlin. There I met Papa's younger brother Zalmen. He was tall, handsome, and only about twenty years old at the time of our visit. Zalmen took me to meet two little girls, sisters Rosa and Sissel, who were distantly related to our family. Fortunately these girls spoke fairly fluent German, so we had no problem talking together. I spent a happy afternoon playing with them. Rosa asked me if I knew how to give a "Butterfly Kiss".

When I said I did not, she put her face close to mine, our cheeks touching, and fluttered her eyelids. This caused her eyelashes to give my cheek a tickling sensation. Rosa and Sissel—and the Butterfly Kiss—are a poignant memory of two little girls who disappeared in the turmoil of the approaching war.

Every year in Berlin, at Passover, the aunts I met in Bialystok sent us a large parcel with handmade Matzo from a local Jewish baker. Silvia and I eagerly looked forward to this treat every Passover festival.

Another journey Papa and I took together was when I was eleven. We spent two weeks in Spindlermuehle, Czechoslovakia, a winter resort, where Papa knew I could skate every day to my heart's content. One memorable afternoon, Papa and I went hiking in the hills around the resort. When we reached a particularly isolated stretch of the snowy hiking trail, Papa said, "Watch this!"

He took his alpine hiking stick, and in the flat field of freshly fallen snow, using his stick, he started to write something in huge letters. Soon I could see on the white surface the words he had written "HITLER VERECKE!" (Hitler drop dead). I was so proud of him, but at the same time couldn't wait to get away from this incriminating piece of graffiti. I recall his glee at being able to do this without fear of punishment. For hours afterwards, each time we looked at each other, he'd wink at me and I'd start to giggle. He said, "This will be our secret forever."

Papa and I took skiing lessons in a group organized by our hotel. Unfortunately, this was our last carefree time together until after we escaped from Germany in 1939.

Chapter Eight

Berlin 1936
Hundekehle

We often spent Sunday afternoons in the summer at the outdoor recreation facility called "Hundekehle" (Dog's Throat), a short drive from Berlin. I have no idea why this lovely country restaurant had such an odd name. It was the preferred destination where my parents and their friends could get together at the tables set under the trees, and have 'Kaffee und Kuchen" in the fresh air, while we children played at the nearby pond and fed the ducks.

Mutti's brother, my Onkel Grischa, with his wife Tante Mia and their two little boys, often met us there for a carefree afternoon of visiting and socializing. Even though this was a country destination, it was an occasion for really getting dressed up. Mutti wore a pretty flower-printed chiffon dress, with matching wide-brimmed hat and high heeled shoes, while Papa wore a suit and tie. Silvia and I were togged out in matching dresses sewn by Mutti. We were reminded frequently: "Keep them clean!"

While the adults sipped strong coffee and nibbled on whipped cream cakes, we children were served Bluemchen Kaffee—(Blossom coffee). This meant coffee so weak that the flower decorations inside the cups were clearly visible through the watery beverage. As the oldest child present, I was delegated to take care of Silvia, and my cousins Wolfgang and Ralf, Grisha's sons. I discovered I had a talent for frightening the two little boys by telling them ghost stories. Their favorite was an invention of mine about the ducks that were peacefully paddling in the pond with their retinue of little baby ducklings in V-formations trailing them.

I made up a scary story about these ducks, telling my sister and little cousins that the ducks were haunted, and had special powers, which caused the children to run crying back to the table where the grown-ups sat enjoying their day of respite from the constant worries of living in Berlin. I learned how to put on an innocent expression and shrug my shoulders when the two boys ran to their mother and hid their faces in her lap.

I had known and liked Mia's family all my life. Her brother, Onkel Ignatz once had a long conversation with me on the art of making a perfect tomato sandwich. I was very impressed that he took the time to talk to me about such a 'grown-up' subject as tomato sandwiches. And Mia's sister Meta—beautiful, elegant Tante Meta—once came into our kitchen while Mutti was frying potato pancakes for the festival of Chanukah. Meta asked Mutti what she was cooking. When Mutti told her 'Latkes'—the Yiddish word for potato pancakes—Meta's unforgettable comment was: "Ach, wie apart !" (Oh, how unusual !)

Mia's youngest sister Tante Ernie frequently joined us in these peaceful and happy afternoons. I liked Ernie a lot, not only because she wasn't much taller than I, but also because she had wonderful twinkling black eyes, and told very funny jokes and stories to us children. We loved to be in her company and were always delighted to see her. She often wore a small hat at a jaunty angle with a dotted veil that fell over her face. This lent Ernie an air of mystery totally at odds with her sunny personality.

Sunday afternoons at Hundekehle with their touch of glamour and family fun are some of the memories I cherish. They were much needed respites from the tension and fear that were so overwhelming for Jewish Berliners in the 1930s.

Chapter Nine

Berlin 1936
Shoshana and Shayndel

My aunt Shoshana was Mutti's youngest sibling. She had emigrated from Bialystok with her father, my Opa Simcha, to Holon, a suburb of Haifa, in Palestine. The whole family had a strong Zionist orientation, and my Opa was fulfilling a life-long dream by emigrating to the Holy Land. When Shoshana finished high school in Palestine, she decided to study Nursing with a special emphasis on newborn babies.

She knew that the best school for her purpose was a famous Nursing Institute in Berlin. So she came from Holon to stay with us in Berlin and study Nursing. Her German was fluent, so we had no problem communicating with our lively young aunt who was so excited at being in the sophisticated environment of Berlin. She didn't have too much spare time from her studies, but I remember some fun-filled times with this pretty, carefree young Tante, whom we called Shanne, like Mutti did. She loved taking us on shopping excursions, particularly to Silvia's and my favorite destination, the huge department store in the center of Berlin called Ka-De-We.

Tante Shanne's time in Berlin was cut short because one of her fellow students told the school authorities that Shanne was a Jew. She had not mentioned this on her application because the Nazis were already putting restrictions on Jewish education. She was immediately dismissed, and consequently returned to Palestine with the plans for her career completely derailed. Fifty years later, when I visited Israel and stayed with Shanne for several weeks, she told me of her intense anger and disappointment at having been denounced by a fellow student.

She still regretted not having had a chance to fulfill her plans for a career in nursing. She told me that the Nursing School in Berlin had established a quota system for Jewish students. Unfortunately for Shanne, the quota had already been filled for that year. After Shoshana returned to Palestine, my father's youngest sister arrived in Berlin from Bialystok. Shayndel was about 19 years old and was determined to study Fashion Design and pattern-making in Berlin. Her name Shayndel Rozanski obviously did not set off any warning bells of "Jewishness" in the Berlin Fashion Institute where she registered as a student. She stayed with us and was, like Tante Shoshana before her, a very welcome addition to Silvia's and my life in Berlin.

She had sparkling black eyes, a great sense of humor, and liked singing the latest German song hits, "Schlager", and grabbing me to dance around our living room. She told us of her handsome boyfriend who was waiting for her in Bialystok, how much she loved him, and how she could hardly bear to be separated from him.

Shayndel and Papa, her oldest brother, had a very warm and loving relationship. She also brought a special sense of fun into Mutti's life. My mother was already starting to think about emigrating from Germany if she could manage to locate a country that would be willing to accept us. Shayndel loved the movies and on Saturday mornings took Silvia and me to see Shirley Temple films whenever possible. She got the giggles when Cinema ushers walked up and down the aisles, using huge spray guns to shoot heavily perfumed air over the seated movie goers. She also took me along on a shopping quest one day, wanting desperately to buy a pair of red shoes for herself. She thought these were the height of cosmopolitan elegance and said that she'd stop traffic in Bialystok when she returned and wore them there.

Because she was studying Dressmaking, she started to make a fashionable wardrobe for Silvia's doll. Silvia did not appreciate this at all. Her doll had been bought by Mutti in Czechoslovakia and it wore the traditional folk costume of that country that included lots of embroidered frills and a white lace blouse. Silvia did not want her doll to look like a fashionable Berliner. There were entreaties and tears. Shayndel wound up making a suit of some kind for my Teddy bear.

I don't remember the reason for Shayndel's rather hasty departure. I think her boyfriend somehow was involved in her decision. I never saw my lively and pretty aunt again. She, together with her sisters, my other aunts, was locked up in the Bialystok Ghetto when the Germans occupied Poland in 1939. Then later they all were shipped to Treblinka, the concentration camp halfway between Warsaw and Bialystok. My father learned of her terrible death in that camp from some survivors, who contacted him after the war and gave him the details of how his sisters were misused by German soldiers, and finally died of disease and starvation. Each time such a letter arrived at our flat in London, I heard my father's sobs and then saw him sitting Shivah on a small bench in our living room. Silvia and I tiptoed about, not knowing how to comfort him.

Shoshana survived because she chose Palestine for her home. Shayndel perished miserably because she had never even tried to leave her family.

Chapter Ten

Berlin 1937
The Concert

Mutti's friend Frau Felczer was a frequent visitor at our apartment on Niebuhr Strasse. She and my mother often spent time fitting dresses on each other. With both women being adept seamstresses, I don't think they ever wore ready-made clothes from a store. They enjoyed these fitting get-togethers because of a love for fashion and beautiful fabrics.

I liked to sit quietly watching how these two close friends developed style and fit. One afternoon Mutti was trying on a long gown with Frau Felczer helping with the fitting. With a tuck here, a fold and a twist there, the garment suddenly came alive. What a wondrous talent to make this shimmering velvet fabric into a gown that turned Mutti into a queen. Impressed with this skill, I decided then and there I would learn it too.

A few evenings later, Mutti and Papa dressed to attend a Richard Tauber performance, the last time they would be able to attend the theater where Jewish patrons were still welcome. Mutti was resplendent in the beautiful velvet gown she and Frau Felczer had created only a few days before. Before leaving for the theater, Papa set up his camera and tripod and posed Mutti in her velvet gown. Then he did the trick with the self-timer and ran to her side to proudly pose in his tuxedo before the camera clicked.

That photo is now a treasured memento in my family album. It is significant because, after that evening, their lives no longer involved getting dressed up and going out on formal occasions.

Papa became a truck driver when we escaped to England, and Mutti took in sewing by piecework, yet I never heard any complaint from either of them. We knew we had been incredibly lucky to have escaped as a family, and to have found a haven of security in London. Even though our first home there was two rooms in a bug-infested slum, with mattresses on the floor, and a toilet shared by six families, we knew we were as safe as any other London resident. Best of all, we no longer had to fear sudden Nazi round-ups and deportations.

Chapter Eleven

Berlin 1937
A Christmas Experience

The winter seasons in Berlin were very colorful and exciting. This was largely due to the street markets' displays of Christmas themes that appeared in every neighborhood. The "Weihnachtsmarkt" near us had brightly lit booths and stalls that overflowed with glittering trimmings for the fragrant pine trees that were on sale in each market. How I envied the children who were allowed to buy—and eat— the little pink marzipan piglets that were a symbol of good luck in Germany. The marzipan was just a sugar and almond concoction, but because it was in the shape of pigs, Silvia and I were not permitted to buy or eat these tempting goodies.

I also admired the Advent Calendars with their mysterious little doors to be opened one at a time every day for a month before Christmas. Little surprises were hidden behind each of these doors. I was so envious of the children who were given these wonderful objects. Mutti realized how much I wanted to experience this totally foreign festival. So she asked our building superintendent Herr Bollmann to invite Silvia and me into his home to see their Christmas tree.

One evening Mutti took us to the Bollmann apartment. We were invited in by Frau Bollmann and her son Horst. I was not prepared for the sight of the tall, fragrant pine tree draped with silver streamers, and with the little wax candles clipped to the branches. The various kinds of ornaments—hand-blown glass birds with spun-glass tails, little elves, colored globes—surprised me. I had never seen anything like them.

The bowls of Pfeffernuesse—their aroma so tempting—remained not tasted. Mutti had asked us not to eat anything in this household. She was sure everything was baked in lard. So we just sat and gazed at this miraculous tree. Herr Bollmann lit the candles and lowered the lights in the room. He, his wife and son sang several carols for us. They were decent, kind people and did not respond to others who told them to hate and fear Jews. I knew this couple stood for values and manners that were sadly lacking in most of the other Berliners we met.

When Herr Foerster took over our apartment, and we had to leave, the Bollmann family came to say goodbye to us. I heard Frau Bollmann whispering to Mutti, "What can we do about the Fuehrer? After all, he put bread on our tables." They had permitted Horst to play with us. He was our only non-Jewish playmate. And I know now what a risk they took then. Good people, fondly remembered, with gratitude.

Chapter Twelve

Berlin 1937
Mixed Marriages

Among my parents' friends was a couple who lived near us in the Charlottenburg section of Berlin. Herbert, a tall, handsome man, was Jewish, and his wife Ursula, a petite blonde who was always elegantly dressed, was Christian. Because of a Nazi edict concerning "Mixed Marriages" this couple was ordered to divorce because he was "dishonoring" a pure Aryan woman. Being very much in love, they refused to follow this order, so Herbert was arrested and sent to the recently opened Dachau Concentration camp for a six-month correction and punishment period.

When Herbert returned to Berlin, he visited my parents one afternoon to tell them about his stay in the camp. I was sitting on the sofa in our living room reading. My mother told me to leave the room before Herbert started to tell his story, but my father insisted that I stay, saying: "Let her hear— let her remember." So I closed my book, joined the adults at the table and heard what Herbert had to tell.

His head was shaved as soon as he arrived at the camp. It was demeaning to lose his dark, curly hair, but worse treatment was to follow. He was forced to hang a cardboard sign around his neck that proclaimed in large letters: **I HAVE DEFILED AND RAPED A PURE ARYAN WOMAN** ! He was also given a hand bell to ring as he walked around the camp to call attention to this proclamation.

Unlike the other Jewish prisoners, this group was denied access to eating utensils. Their gruel was poured into bowls placed on the ground, and had to be eaten on all fours— the way dogs eat.

On his return to Berlin, he and Ursula reunited. His hair had not yet fully grown back when they came to our apartment to say Goodbye. They had managed to obtain a visa and were emigrating to Argentina.

Chapter Thirteen

Berlin 1937
KaDeWe—The Department Store

In the 1930s, we always lived within walking distance of the fabulous department store in the heart of Berlin, KaDeWe. The full name was actually "Kaufhaus Des Westens" meaning "Store of the West." We all called it KaDeWe, and a shopping trip with Mutti to this famed store was a regular event. She always took Silvia and me with her, usually to the sixth floor, which was a glorious Food Court that had, till about 1937, a kosher section.

We always hoped that Mutti would take her time picking and choosing the Kosher tidbits for our weekend meals. While she shopped, Silvia and I sped off to all the forbidden counters which offered free samples of the most delicious, but non-kosher, meat products, and cheeses.

One attraction was the highly colored jelly molds in vivid reds and greens called "Goetterspeise" ("Food of the Gods"). Served for sampling in tiny pleated paper cups, with a wooden spoon stuck into it, this jelly's quivering, shimmering mass drew our attention. Mutti was convinced these jellies were made from a product of the bones of horses. This made it even more attractive to Silvia and me. We simply had to sample what a horse tasted like. The Wurst slices, most generously offered to us, were delicious. We happily picked from the artfully arranged samples on big platters for customers to taste. We scurried from counter to counter, giggling and trying to hide our activity from Mutti. I think she knew exactly what we were doing but didn't have the heart to stop our fun.

Another department at KaDeWe that totally fascinated me was the cosmetics and perfume counters on the main floor. I loved to watch elegant young women try on lipsticks and drip perfume on their wrists. Oh how I wanted to be just like them! But my "coming of age" was to be in London, with bombs dropping all around, sleeping in air raid shelters and wearing clothing bought with English pounds sterling and ration coupons.

The thrill of visiting KaDeWe was enhanced by the fact that near the main entrance was a wall fountain that spurted a stream of delicious orangeade, a definite sweet magnet for the children of customers. There were little cone-shaped paper cups in a dispenser next to this miraculous fountain.

Silvia and I made ourselves ill a few times, gorging on the forbidden food samples upstairs and, before leaving the store, asking Mutti if we could stop to drink that heavenly orangeade. I don't remember seeing any anti-Jewish placards in the store or in the display windows. I assume the store had some Jewish people among its owners.

Nor do I remember any broken windows or merchandise being thrown from KaDeWe into the street during Kristall Nacht. Maybe the Nazis realized how important this store was to the image of Berlin as a world class cosmopolitan center of German culture and commerce.

Our carefree and happy afternoons at KaDeWe came to an abrupt end when we had to move from our apartment on Niebuhr Strasse to make way for Herr Foerster. From then on we lived in one room in the Levent's apartment, and Mutti shared the kitchen with Frau Levent. There was no time or room for anything but the most basic meals and no more visits to that fabled Food Court to sample the forbidden goodies.

Chapter Fourteen

Berlin 1938
The Poison Rings

I remember a gold signet ring Papa wore with his initials engraved on its top. When he first wore this ring, I was so impressed that I told my best friend Hannah about it.

She asked, "Is it a poison ring?"

This made no sense to me. I asked, "What do you mean, 'poison ring'?"

Hannah explained that her older sister had told her that many Jews now wore poison rings. She said that in a small cavity under an ornamental top several tiny white pills of cyanide could be concealed. The top of the ring was designed to swivel open when a hidden spring was pressed, giving the ring wearer access to the poison.

Her Uncle Heinz wore such a ring. He had told her that if the Nazis ever came for him, he would not let himself be arrested and taken to a concentration camp. He said he'd swallow the little white pills and die immediately. She also told me that most of the grown ups she knew were having these rings made for use in just such an emergency.

I was worried. When I came home from school that day, I asked my father to take off his ring and let me look at it. He knew why I'd asked. He laughed and said, "Don't worry. It's not a poison ring. I wouldn't do that to my family and leave you alone in an emergency".

He removed it and offered it to me. Carefully examining the heavy gold ring, I could find no evidence of a secret compartment. I later looked up the word "cyanide" in our dictionary and learned that when this poison is taken in sufficient quantity it results in an agonizing death. Every day from then on, I carefully checked my parents' hands to be sure they were not wearing poison rings.

These rings eventually became a topic of conversation at social gatherings where some of our friends actually showed off this newly purchased jewelry with its deadly secret. It occurs to me that I now seek out and wear very large ornamental rings as a reminder of those grim times.

Papa's gold ring is now in Silvia's possession. When she and I were dividing my parents' jewelry after Mutti's death in 1980, I was glad to let my sister take it.

Chapter Fifteen

Berlin, November 1938
Wilhelm Kruetzfeld

One of Papa's close friends was the man whom Silvia
and I called "Onkel Wilhelm". His full title and name was
Polizei Oberleutnant Wilhelm Kruetzfeld. Papa and he had
been friends for years. This friendship continued even after
Onkel Wilhelm was forced to join the Nazi party to keep his
job as police lieutenant.

He didn't come to visit very often. That would have been
too dangerous for him, but I do recall long phone conversations
between Papa and Onkel. One evening, a very short and
abrupt call came from him. He told my father not to ask any
questions, just leave our apartment immediately, take no
luggage, and to stay away for two days. Without saying
anything, Papa understood. It was November, so Papa put
on his overcoat. He told me to take care of Mutti and Silvia,
kissed us all, and hurriedly left. The next morning our
doorbell rang. There stood three young men in the dreaded
brown Nazi uniforms, holding pistols, asking to see my father.

My mother said he had just left for work. They proceeded to search our apartment, even looking under the beds and in the closets. They told my trembling mother that they would return, and they did, that afternoon, again searching and poking into every corner.

Papa returned two days later. The newspapers reported that day a just-concluded successful action of rounding up Jewish men of Polish nationality. Papa never told Mutti where he hid during that time, but I know their efforts to leave Germany intensified after those searches. Urgent letters were sent to distant relatives in America, and to Papa's school friend from Bialystok who now lived in Paris.

My parents spent most of their time and energy going from one foreign embassy to another, standing in long lines, seeking entry visas, only to be assigned yet another quota number. They hoped for a miracle every day until the mail came and there were no visas from any of the countries' embassies that my parents had applied to.

After the war, I read that Herr Kruetzfeld had been recognized as a Quiet Hero. He had saved the lives of forty Jewish Berliners, risking his own life and the lives of his family by making those fateful telephone calls.

Chapter Sixteen

Berlin 1938
Kristallnacht

When I got up the morning of November 9, 1938, Mutti told me not to go out into the street. During the night a big "ACTION" by the Nazis had taken place against the Jewish residents of all of Germany, not just in Berlin. The radio announcer reported that all Jewish houses of worship had been set on fire and were going up in flames. Our beautiful synagogues had their ornate and colorful stained glass windows smashed by rifle butts wielded by SS officers, and the Eternal flames that lit the Arks in intricately wrought bronze lanterns were extinguished and destroyed. The Torah scrolls had been pulled from their Arks, and had been unrolled, ripped and trampled. Our treasured prayer books had been tossed into the flames by cheering Hitler Youths, urged on by the jeering onlookers whose happy faces later appeared in Newsreels at the local cinema.

I wanted to go outside to see what was happening, but Mutti was adamant about keeping Silvia and me indoors.

Finally I persuaded Papa to take me outside—he always said he wanted me to "see and remember"—so, clutching his hand, I walked over with him to the Kurfuersten Damm. The "Kudamm" was the major shopping area of Berlin, lined with boutiques and specialty shops, many of which were operated by their Jewish owners. We found the wide sidewalks covered with glistening shards of glass from the smashed shop windows that had been bashed in during the night.

The stores' merchandise was strewn all over the street. I saw jubilant Nazis calling the bewildered shop owners "Judenschweine" kicking them and forcing them to their knees, making them pick up the broken glass with their bare hands. I was horrified watching this unbelievable scene while tightly gripping my father's hand. Papa's face was pale and grim. Speaking softly, he kept reminding me not to make a sound. Tears ran silently down my cheeks.

The broken glass crunched under our shoes as we returned to our apartment on Niebuhr Strasse. When I calmed down, I told my mother that I needed a new pair of shoes with much thicker soles because of the strange sensation of walking on broken glass. I worried that the shards of glass would slice through the soles of my shoes and cut my feet.

Silvia's school, which was attached to a synagogue, was completely destroyed and never reopened. My school was closed by the Nazis and as a result I had to travel across Berlin every day to attend the one centrally located Jewish High School on Wilsnacker Strasse that remained open. This overcrowded school was in a state of turmoil and transition. Almost every week we had new teachers as Jewish instructors were either being arrested and shipped to concentration camps or managed somehow to escape Germany.

The Nazis maintained strict records of High School attendance. Jewish parents who kept their children home from school were often interrogated and punished. My parents had no trouble keeping Silvia at home because she flatly refused to attend school or to even go out into the streets. They obtained a medical certificate for her that stated she had a skin infection making it impossible for her to attend school.

The Nazis later announced that Jewish business owners would not receive payments of damage claims from their insurance companies. All such money had to be turned over to the State to help clean up the"mess" caused by the business owners creating the hazard of broken glass on the sidewalks.

Needless to say, the affected businesses were permanently closed and their owners, many of them now penniless, joined all the other Jewish residents of Berlin in frantically trying to find a country anywhere in the world that would permit them to enter and give them sanctuary.

Chapter Seventeen

Berlin 1938
Herr Foerster

Mutti and I were at home one afternoon in December. Papa was at work and Silvia was visiting a neighbor. Though we were not expecting any visitors, our doorbell rang. Mutti opened the door and there stood a smiling, tall, broad-shouldered, heavyset man in a Nazi uniform. He had two teenaged girls beside him. He politely introduced himself as Herr Foerster, and the girls as his daughters. He told Mutti that he had come to survey our apartment to decide what he would want to "purchase" from us.

I knew my parents had no intention of selling our possessions. We were hoping to emigrate and take everything with us to our new home. I started to tell Herr Foerster that there must be some mistake, but Mutti gave me a warning look and put her finger to her lips, so reluctantly I kept silent.

One of Herr Foerster's daughters carried a clipboard and a pencil, and, as they slowly strolled from room to room, her father would point at a piece of furniture, a painting, or to my mother's cherished Oriental rugs. He made sure that his clipboard-carrying daughter carefully wrote down everything he pointed to.

He obviously liked our dining room furniture, particularly admiring the sideboard that Mutti polished so carefully every week. Nothing escaped his notice. Mutti asked him if she could keep her sewing machine, and he graciously consented. She also asked him if we could keep a chiming mantle clock that Papa liked to tinker with. Again he agreed with a smile.

In Silvia's and my bedroom, his daughters noticed Silvia's favorite doll—a souvenir from my mother's trip to a Czechoslovakian spa a few years before. The doll was entered on the clipboard list as was my beloved teddy bear that slept on my bed each night. By then I was practically holding my breath in order not to raise any objection to the "buying trip" of this large, genial Nazi officer who really liked my parents' taste in furniture.

When his list was complete, Mutti had to sign each page. She was handed carbon copies and admonished to have every listed item in the apartment in place when Herr Foerster and his family moved in. We were given a date by which we had to leave our home. We were fortunate to find a room with the Levents, our German-Jewish friends.

Herr Levent had been an officer in the German army in the "Great War" of 1914-1918 (WW-I). He displayed his medals for bravery proudly in a shadowbox frame on the living room wall. The Levents, an elderly couple, were convinced that his war record would protect them, and prevent them from being deported to the Auschwitz concentration camp.

Before we left for Hamburg and England, the Levents asked us to take a wedding gift to their daughter, who had previously escaped to London. Silvia and I were to present to Irene Levent an antique lace wedding handkerchief, which had belonged to her great-grandmother, and had been carried at the wedding of every Levent bride for as long as

Frau Levent could remember. Silvia and I were to wear the silver-painted cardboard angels' wings, which Frau Levent had purchased for this special occasion, tied to our shoulders as winged messengers from her loving parents in Berlin. They may have sensed they would never see their daughter again. Frau Levent wrote a poem for the presentation and she taught it to Silvia and me.

A few days after we arrived in London, Mutti took us on the Underground to visit Irene. We stood in front of her, with the angels' wings tied to our shoulders, reciting the poem Irene's mother had written in Berlin just a few days before.

Irene cried. Mutti cried, and Silvia and I were relieved to have remembered every word of the poem, and made a successful presentation of the Levent family heirloom just the way Irene's mother had planned.

[After the war, we heard that both of the Levents had been arrested, and shipped to a death camp in a cattle car without any seats or facilities. Because of their advanced age, they were immediately murdered in the gas chamber.]

Chapter Eighteen

Berlin 1938
Yellow Benches and Chocolate Cake

My friend Daisy arrived in school one day in 1938 with an expression I've since heard called "like a cat that just swallowed the canary". In other words, she was extremely pleased about something. She leaned over to me and, with a big smile, whispered that she had an announcement to make. She raised her hand, then stood up without waiting to be acknowledged by the teacher, and blurted out, "I have a new brother named Bobby." She proudly added, "Now I am a big sister."

Naturally, I was intrigued with her baby brother. I offered to accompany Daisy one sunny afternoon when she took her little brother to nearby Tiergarten Park in his baby carriage. Mutti had started teaching me to embroider, so I took my tablecloth with the pattern printed on it, to work on while we were sitting in the park with Bobby in his pram.

Something different was glaringly apparent as we entered this lovely park. Several of the park benches had been painted a brilliant yellow. Stencilled across the top of each yellow bench was a sentence in large black letters that read: RESERVED FOR JEWS. A Star of David appeared at each end of this sentence.

By silent agreement, Daisy and I sat on one of these yellow benches to enjoy the beautiful day. I took out my embroidery and was soon engrossed in stitching the leaves and flowers the way Mutti had taught me. Daisy and I were lucky that day because there were very few Berliners and no uniformed Nazis in the park. Passers-by looked away in embarrassment apparently not enjoying the sight of two little girls sitting on a yellow bench marked specifically for Jews.

That very tablecloth now covers my kitchen table. Every meal I set on it, reminds me of the yellow bench, the sunny afternoon and my friend Daisy. She now lives in Israel, is a great-grandmother, and her "baby" brother Bobby is a grandfather. I wonder if she remembers that day with the same emotions that I still experience.

Another memory also involves Daisy. Her mother gave a birthday party for her every year and served the most delicious chocolate cake that she baked only for this occasion. She kept the recipe secret and refused to share it, not even with my mother. This rich chocolate cake also had a strong lemon flavor. Silvia and I often pleaded with Mutti to duplicate this marvelous birthday cake for our birthdays. She tried to bake it once or twice, but never could equal Mrs. Rubin's famous chocolate-lemon birthday cake.

Chapter Nineteen

Berlin 1938
The Skating Skirt

A winter evening in 1938 remains clear in my memory. It was on that evening that my future took a very specific direction. This was the result of our friends, the Felczers' visit. Mutti had a problem. She had promised to design and sew a skating skirt for Silvia just like the ones worn by professional ice skaters. We had always gone skating in our "Trainings Anzuege" that were shapeless, fuzzy jogging outfits with ballooning pants. Because we skated at an outdoor rink, which really was a tennis court that was flooded in freezing weather, Mutti thought we'd be warmer if we wore those heavy, but cozy outfits.

Silvia rebelled against her shapeless costume. She wanted to look stylish like a real ice dancer. Mutti had not been able to find a pattern for such a skirt in the few stores that still allowed Jewish customers to enter. So she phoned her friend who was a professional designer and seamstress.

The Felczers came over for a visit that evening and brought their daughter Ina. Quickly Silvia and Ina disappeared into our bedroom to play with dolls. Papa took Herr Felczer into his office which was adjacent to our living room, no doubt to discuss the situation facing all Jewish Berliners.

Mutti and Frau Felczer got down to the business of making a skating skirt while I watched. I remember the glittering chandelier lighting our dining table where Mutti and Frau Felczer worked. Frau Felczer picked up the green velvet fabric that Silvia had insisted on. She folded it in a special way, then, with a tape measure and a piece of narrow-edged tailor's chalk in hand, she swiftly drew a few lines on the fabric, cut along those lines, and suddenly she held in her hands a beautiful, graceful circular skirt. It only needed some minor stitching to become a gorgeous skating outfit for Silvia. To me it was a miracle.

Frau Felczer saw my amazement. I asked, "How did you do that?" While it seemed like magic to me, Frau Felczer smiled and said that if I wanted to know how to do this, I could learn dress design and pattern-making. Then I, too, would be able to draw lines on a piece of fabric, cut it out, and create a wonderful garment. I decided right then that this was what I wanted to do when I grew up—other than designing houses and villas in my dreams. My focus never changed after that evening. I have designed wedding dresses, formal gowns, and lingerie. I have never regretted choosing this path.

Unfortunately, by the time Mutti finished sewing the skating skirt for Silvia, the Ice Rink had posted a sign forbidding Jews to use this facility.

Chapter Twenty

Berlin 1938
Lisa

I remember Lisa well because at the age of twelve she had already distinguished herself in our school Adass Yisroel by being one of the fastest competitive runners at our yearly Maccabi sports events. The Maccabi games were arranged by the Jewish school system to give us youngsters an opportunity to compete in sports and to disprove Goebbels' references to all Jews as fat, clumsy parasites of the Aryan nation of Germany.

Lisa was tall, slim, and an incredibly fast runner, winning medals and ribbons for our school every time she ran competitively. I always felt she was barely aware of me. I was the shortest girl in class and fairly clumsy at gymnastics. We were not exactly friends. She was usually surrounded by a group of admiring girls, while I hung back, just glad that she was in my class at school.

Our reunion took place in the spring of the year 2000 on board a Lufthansa flight from New York to Berlin. We were members of a group of former refugees who had been invited by the Berlin city government to return, as its guests, for an 8-day visit to the city of our birth. Lisa and I had not seen each other for 60 years. In fact, I had no idea that she had survived the Holocaust, nor that she was now living in New York City, virtually around the corner from my sister Silvia.

Before the trip all participants had been supplied with a list of our fellow passengers. When I saw the name Lisa Klein, Manhattan, I got out my New York City telephone book and looked up her number. In great anticipation I asked the woman who answered my call if she was the Lisa Klein who had been the fastest runner in our school. When she said yes, we both could not believe that after 60 years we had reconnected. Both of us had been turning down the annual invitation by the Mayor's office of Berlin. It was fortuitous that we both had decided, in the year 2000, to finally accept the free trip to return on a visit.

Lisa and I have since become good friends. Now we are both involved in writing our memoirs of that distant, turbulent time during our childhood when we never knew from day-to-day what was going to happen to our schoolmates and friends.

Chapter Twenty-One

Berlin 1939
Rabbi Rebhuhn

Jewish children had long been forbidden to attend public schools in Berlin for fear of tainting our Aryan fellow students with our religious beliefs. Addas Yisroel, the school I attended in 1938, was a Jewish school much like a Yeshiva.

This school was staffed mainly by orthodox teachers, even Rabbis. Looking back now I realize our class of rambunctious twelve-year-old girls must have been a challenging assignment for these men of God, and particularly for our homeroom teacher Rabiner Doktor Rebhuhn. Herr Doktor was an enthusiastic, vigorous young man in his twenties. We must have often tested his patience and his devotion to Judaism.

One of us claimed that she had discovered that orthodox Jewish men were not supposed to look directly into the eyes of girls or women, except those who were family members. So, of course, it became a challenge to the entire class to try to get him to look into our eyes.

Sitting in class, we would all stare at Doktor Rebhuhn, trying to get into his line of vision, even leaning over and contorting ourselves. Only a few of us girls were from orthodox homes. Most of us came from liberal, almost assimilated families, and were attending this school because we were excluded from the Public school system. Doktor Rebhuhn was really challenged to keep us in order.

Edith, a particularly willful and assertive girl, told us before class one day that she had figured out a way to make Herr Doktor blush. She wouldn't tell us how she planned to do this, so we were all very attentive when she raised her hand to ask a question during Bible study class. When Herr Doktor called on her, she stood up and asked her fateful question. "Please, Herr Doktor, why can't Jewish girls be circumcised like Jewish boys?" The question was so unexpected, we were shocked into total silence. But then we all burst into laughter.

Poor Herr Doktor! God must have been watching over him. He was saved by the class bell. Edith became our heroine of the day. I believe he gave her a letter to take home to her parents requesting that her father sign it. I don't remember the repercussions of this prank.

Recently, I received a letter from my friend Daisy in Israel. She had visited a Kibbutz and had seen the name "Rebhuhn" among the list of its residents. She asked to meet him and he turned out to be the younger brother of our Rabiner Doktor Rebhuhn. Daisy told him that she had been in the Rabbi's class in Berlin. His brother said Herr Doktor had been sent to Auschwitz and murdered.

This elderly man's big regret was that he had no mementos and no keepsakes of his brother. Daisy promised him she would contact other class members to see if anyone had souvenirs of that time in Doktor Rebhuhn's class.

When I received Daisy's letter I remembered that I still had my Poesy Album with notes in it from most of my teachers. I recalled that Dr. Rebhuhn had written something for me in it, both in Hebrew and in German. I located the little album, and sent a photocopy of this page to Daisy in Israel. She forwarded it to Doktor's brother on the kibbutz. His brother received this more than fifty years after Doktor's tragic death. Daisy and I were so gratified that we had been able to help bring a sense of closure to the brother who was still grieving the loss of his sibling in that hellish place.

Chapter Twenty-Two

School Vacation 1938
Summer Camp in Denmark

During school vacations, my parents did not want Silvia and me to spend our days in the parks and streets of Berlin. There was no option for vacations of any kind for Jewish families. All hotels and resorts advertised "JUDEN UNERWUENSCHT", a phrase meaning: "JEWS NOT WANTED". Their only choice was to send us out of Germany to one of several Jewish Holiday camps available only to children included in a temporary group-visa.

My parents decided on a camp in Denmark run by two Jewish women, the Fleischer sisters, Ruth and Renate. They were fat, unpleasant spinsters, and to Silvia and me, they came to represent pure evil. They took advantage of the fact that our parents would not be able to visit us because adult visitors' visas to Denmark were not available.

These two harridans rented a decrepit farm on the Island of Bornholm in Denmark, and promised Jewish Berliners that their children would have a carefree, safe and happy holiday, away from the constant threat of Nazi harassment. When our group arrived at the "Holiday Camp", we found several large barns, drafty and leaking, with triple-tiered wooden bunks and hard thin mattresses. The dining room was in another dirty barn that had rough trestle-tables and splintery benches. The food was the worst I had ever eaten.

We were forced to finish all the food on our plates that had been doled out to us with a huge, rusty ladle dipped from an iron cauldron on wheels. If we didn't clean our plates, we had to sit at the table until we did finish the pungent mess. These two greedy, unprincipled women had us totally at their mercy.

There was no program of activities. Instead, every morning we were driven in a large open-backed truck to a small beach. All of us got blistery sunburns, as well as foot infections from the rough sand and pebbles. I actually yearned for the streets of Berlin even with all the dangers those streets held for Jewish children.

One morning my stomach rebelled against the grey slimy gruel dumped on our plates for breakfast. I started retching and heaving. I was permitted to leave the table and run to the privy, but Fraeulein Renate called after me, "Come right back and finish your breakfast when you feel better." That day the truck took the campers to the beach as usual except for me. I had to stay behind, and sit with my plate of breakfast porridge congealing in front of me until I'd eaten it, which I adamantly refused to do.

The sisters relented at lunch time. I was allowed to leave the table after consuming the sausages and boiled cabbage that were our usual midday meal. I wrote letter after letter to my parents in Berlin, but they never received any of them. Our letters were carefully screened, and if they contained any negative remarks, they were not mailed. A general newsletter, sent out once a week to the parents, told of how much fun we were all having and how we were enjoying the fresh air and wholesome food.

We discovered a patch of wild blueberries in an adjacent grove of trees, and often sneaked over to pick handfuls of these delicious berries to supplement our diet. A local farmer also let us into his apple orchard to help him pick his crop of sour green fruit. Of course we were so hungry that we ate some of the apples while picking them.

Unfortunately for us, the fruit had been sprayed with a strong bug killer, which we soon learned about when we all came down with violent stomach cramps. One of the girls, who was currying favor with Ruth Fleischer, told her that I had urged the other kids to eat the apples. She singled me out for a nightmarish punishment. She forced me to stand in the center of a circle formed by the other campers. They were then given apples and urged to throw them at me

The trip back to Berlin ended in another mishap. Our parents had been misinformed about the station platform where we would arrive. When Silvia and I got off the train, my parents were not there. The Fleischer sisters, with total disregard for our safety, told me that they would wait exactly three minutes for my parents to show up and then we'd be on our own. Fortunately, Mutti and Papa arrived in time just as the Fleischer sisters picked up their suitcases to leave the station.

When we got home, Mutie gave us a bath. She was horrified to see the bruises all over my body caused by the apples thrown by the children on order of the Fleischer sisters. Mutti told Papa about the bruises. My parents were frustrated. They could do nothing because the sisters were Jewish and there were no lawyers who would sue them for the incompetence and negligence they had shown in supposedly caring for us helpless campers.

To my total amazement, the next Spring, April 1939, the Fleischer sisters came to our home to ask if we'd like to go to camp in Denmark again. I totally lost control. I screamed at these two evil sisters, "I'd rather die than go to one of your vacation camps again!"

Papa took each sister by an elbow and marched them to our front door. As he pushed them out, he said, "Never let me see your faces here again or I won't be responsible for anything I'd do to you!" These two women were well-educated respectable members of the Jewish community. Yet they let greed motivate them when they saw the opportunity to make a great deal of money almost effortlessly.

We didn't go away at all that next summer, our last one in Berlin. Silvia and I spent it at the Levents' apartment, where our family had moved after being forced to leave our home on Niebuhr Strasse. In my spare time, I curled up on the big leather couch in the living room, reading a book I'd discovered on the coffee table, **Vom Winde Verweht (Gone With The Wind)**. In my imagination I was not in Berlin trying to get out, but in Tara, the beautiful mansion with the white columns and the huge porch. I even saw myself wearing a dress with a ruffled skirt and a huge picture hat. It was a pleasant respite to live there in my mind—far from the goose-stepping Nazis, and Hitler's speeches about eradicating undesirable Jews like Mutti and Papa.

Chapter Twenty-Three

Berlin 1938
Hansie Rozanski, Canary

In 1938, when we had to give up our apartment on Niebuhr Strasse and move to a rented room with the Levents on Marburger Strasse, it was quite obvious that, one way or another, we'd be leaving Berlin soon. Silvia and I desperately wanted a pet, either a dog or a cat. But my parents refused because they knew we would not be able to take an animal with us if we managed to escape from Berlin.

Papa told us much later some nightmarish stories of what the Nazis did to "Jewish" cats and dogs whose owners were forced to leave them behind when they were rounded up for shipment to concentration camps.

Still my sister and I kept pleading for a pet. All our negotiating resulted in a little, elderly canary that Papa located somewhere and brought home. He was in a cage with seeds, a cuttlebone, and a little bell. He rewarded us by singing and trilling everyday. Silvia and I were enchanted with this feathery little creature. We called him "Hansie"—little Hans.

Unfortunately, Hansie did not sing for us very long. One morning we found his lifeless body at the bottom of the cage. Silvia and I were devastated. To calm us down and shift our attention from sadness to doing something positive, Papa suggested we give Hansie a proper Jewish burial. We planned and carried out a formal bird burial with Papa's and Mutti's help.

Papa gave us a cigar box, and Mutti helped us pad it with cotton, then line it with blue satin. We placed Hansie into this coffin along with some flowers and his cuttlebone. Because our German neighbors would think it strange for us, the "Juden", to be burying a cigar box in the communal flower bed, Papa suggested we wait until dark before venturing out to bury Hansie.

We all went quietly down in the late evening taking the coffin and a large spatula from the kitchen to dig a grave. Silvia and I reverently placed Hansie's coffin into the hole Mutti had dug. As we were filling it in, Papa whispered the Kaddish—the traditional Hebrew prayer for the dead. In their wisdom, my parents helped us say goodbye to our beloved little pet.

In the year 2000, when I returned to Berlin in a group of guests of the Mayor's Office, one of my intentions was to see again the places where I had lived, and even to visit the garden behind the Post Office on Marburger Strasse, where we had buried Hansie. I went to the old address at Number 12 and walked through the archway into the courtyard, expecting to see the trees and flowers I remembered so well.

Time had marched on. The entire garden had been paved over and was now a parking lot.

Chapter Twenty-Four

Berlin 1938
My First Love

I first met Alexander at Olivaer Platz, a small park in our neighborhood. A group of us used to gather there after school to play Marbles. This was serious business. The marbles were like jewels, glowing colors in shiny glass, and they had special names according to the design within the glass. The most desirable ones were the large "Gala" marbles. They had a lovely gem-like glow in brilliant colors.

The aim was to win and keep as many of these gorgeous spheres as possible. Alexander was a Marbles champion. His bag of marbles was always full of beautiful specimens he had won from the rest of us. He was 13, a year older than I—and had striking blue eyes. No doubt this was the origin of my life-long fascination with blue-eyed men. I have been married three times, each time to a man with brilliant blue eyes. Alexander took very little interest in me, and I was much too shy to approach him. So it was more a case of hero worship than friendship. Alexander also frequented the skating rink where Silvia and I practiced our clumsy figure eights. Of course he was a graceful skater. Just watching him skate was a thrill. I was absolutely overwhelmed when he once treated me to a mug of the hot cocoa that was sold at the little shack where we bought our tickets.

When I hadn't seen Alexander for more than a week, I asked one of his friends where he was. The friend told me Alexander and his family had emigrated to South America. Soon after I lost my first love, we were evicted from our apartment by Herr Foerster and had to move to another section of Berlin. In less than a year, we too, hurriedly left Berlin and escaped to England.

Chapter Twenty-Five

Berlin 1939
Kindertransport

Many of my classmates were sent abroad in the summer of 1939 by desperate parents hoping to save their children from the approaching war in Europe. I remember these school friends with love and sadness. All were saved by their selfless mothers and fathers.

Many of the Kindertransport children, sent for their safety to England, were housed in hostels that were actually orphanages for these frightened, lonely, homesick boys and girls. Often, their most prized possession was a small photo album that had been tucked among their clothes in the single small suitcase they were allowed to take onto the Kindertransport train waiting for them at Anhalter Station in Berlin. When they reached age fourteen, most of these refugee children had to begin working to earn money for their own upkeep. This meant giving up all hope of a higher education.

My friend Paula was sent to England. After the war, she was informed that her whole family—her parents and both brothers—had been murdered in a concentration camp. She emigrated to Australia, eventually married and had two children. She died much too young of cancer.

Hannah, my dear and close friend in school, never saw her parents again. She emigrated after the war to Palestine from London. She settled in Tel Aviv, married, had children, and died of cancer.

Susanne—tall, blond Susie, the daughter of a Berlin Cantor—arrived alone in England. Fortunately her mother managed to escape to England shortly afterwards by signing on as a chambermaid for a small seaside hotel. Her main duty every morning was emptying and cleaning the chamber pots used by hotel guests to relieve themselves during the night.

Susie and her mother went to America about the same time Silvia and I did. She married, raised two children, and also died of cancer. Her father, a cantor with a beautiful voice, had been forced to become a slave laborer in the salt mines near Berlin where he was literally worked to death.

Hanni arrived in London via the Kindertransport program in the summer of 1939. Her parents, the owners of an antiques shop in Berlin, were reluctant to send their only child off to England. She never saw them again.

Right after the war ended in 1945, Hanni met Sigi, also a refugee from Nazi persecution. He and his family had escaped to the USA from Germany in 1939. As soon as Sigi was old enough, he volunteered for the American Army. He was sent to Europe with his unit and, because German was his native language, he became the officer detailed to guard and interrogate the German soldiers who were streaming across the border with their hands raised pleading to be taken prisoners. This he did with a great deal of satisfaction.

On furlough in London, Sigi chanced to meet Hanni who was working for one of his cousins in the fur business. It was "Love at first sight." Hanni soon became one of the many

GI Brides who were transported to the States to marry the American servicemen they had met in Europe.

Hanni and Sigi settled in Westchester just north of New York City and raised two intelligent and gifted children. Once these children were educated, married and independent, Hanni died of cancer. As I was writing this book, Sigi had a massive heart attack in May 2005 and died suddenly in his apartment in Manhattan. He and I had been friends for 50 years and after I became widowed, he tried to cheer me up by e-mailing me two jokes every morning. I will miss my friend Sigi, his loyal friendship and his silly little jokes.

Then there was David, my classmate, with whom I had much in common. He was the shortest boy and I was the smallest girl. He and I were usually picked last for any games where there were "sides". He had a cantorial voice and perfect pitch. Every Friday afternoon, as we filed out of our classroom to go home, our teacher asked him to chant some of the Sabbath prayers. When I said goodbye to my classmates in the summer of 1939, David handed me a bar of chocolate and said, "Don't ever forget me, Ellen."

David and his family had not been able to leave Berlin. In 1940, they were forced into a truck and driven to a railroad siding where they were herded onto a train of cattle cars with other Jewish prisoners already on board. No food or water was supplied to them until they arrived at Auschwitz. He saw his parents and his brother slowly die of overwork and starvation. He was a strong young teenager and, though skin and bones when released by the Allied Army in 1945, managed to survive this ordeal.

Once the war ended, he emigrated to the United States, married, and raised a family. Despite having escaped the death camp, he was never able to overcome his memories of Auschwitz. He finally took his own life by walking to the middle of the George Washington Bridge and leaping to his death in the Hudson River. His body was never found. I learned of his suicide from his widow with whom I spoke after his death. She told me that no matter how she tried to help him, the memories of Auschwitz kept him so depressed that he finally ended his life.

I feel there was a cause-effect in the fate of these survivors. I honor their courage, their lives, and the fact that they survived such impossible situations. The daughters, sent alone to a foreign country at the age of twelve or thirteen, managed to make a life for themselves, and in David's case survived Auschwitz. But after they had raised their children, perhaps they lost the will to go on living.

Some of these girls returned to Berlin in later years on search missions hoping to learn what had happened to their parents. Many of them learned more than enough in Berlin to cause them great sadness for the rest of their lives.

Chapter Twenty-Six

Berlin 1939
Attempting to Learn English

Mutti and Papa were fluent in five languages, Russian, Polish, German, Hebrew and Yiddish. They decided that, since we'd most likely end up in England or America, the family should study English together. They purchased a self-help language system called "Tausend Woerter Englisch" (A Thousand Words of English), which consisted of a set of ten small books contained in a slipcase. These separate booklets allowed all four of us to get involved in this learning project simultaneously.

All of these booklets attempted to teach English via cartoon characters who spoke English transliterated into German pronunciation. The first page of my booklet showed a short, fat man standing opposite a young woman who is holding a tulip in one hand and a rose in the other one. She is saying to him:

> "SOER, DU JU PREFOER DSE TIULIPP TU
> DSE ROOS?"

("Sir, do you prefer the tulip to the rose?")

He responds:

"MADAMM, EI PREFOER JUR TU LIPPS
TU ENNY ROOS!"
("Madam, I prefer your two lips to any rose!")

I practiced and practiced until I could quote the little man and the lady fluently. Another cartoon had the same little fat man demonstrating a large knife to his lady friend.

He is saying:

"SI DSISS NEIF? EI DSHUST BOOT IT."
("See this knife? I just bought it.")

She responds:

"MEI. MEI, HAU SCHARP DSE ETSCH ISS!"
("My, my, how sharp the edge is!")

Our hurried escape to England interrupted all our attempts to learn English. But with a young girl's naivete, I was confident that these two phrases would permit me to start a conversation with anyone in England. My sister Silvia learned another set of silly quotes, while Mutti and Papa were practicing their pointless little conversational phrases together.

To our great disappointment, we were literally "speechless" when we arrived in London and had to forget the 'Tausend Woerter Englisch." It's been over sixty years since I memorized those phrases. When they pop up unexpectedly in my memory, I welcome them as a kind of comic relief to those terrifying last days we spent in the Third Reich.

Chapter Twenty-Seven

Berlin 1939
New Names for Jews

Most of my friends in school were of German nationality. I had a Polish Passport due to my parents having been born in Bialystok, once Russia, now Poland. German law, at that time decreed, that anyone born in Germany of foreign parents, as in my case, was automatically a foreign national. Therefore I was exempt from the new law which compelled every German Jew to carry an identity card at all times.

A particularly cruel and demeaning aspect to these cards was that each owner of such a card was automatically deprived of his or her own first name. All females were renamed "Sara" while all males had to take the name "Israel". The card also had to include a photograph of the bearer, taken in 3/4 view, and exposing the left ear. A theory, expounded by Josef Goebbels, the head of Nazi propaganda, was that one could instantly recognize a Jew by the shape of the ears. If the female being photographed had long hair, it had to be tucked behind the left ear, to fully expose this instant means of racial identification. Of course, none of us paid attention to the edict of calling our friends "Sara"—or "Israel"—and it was a complete mystery to me how one could be deprived of one's name that had been given at birth.

We heard rumors that soon all Jews would have to sew a yellow Star of David onto all their outer garments, either on the right sleeve or over the heart. I became really concerned, not only for myself, but for my sister. Because she had blond curly hair and green eyes, she had been able to walk and play unmolested in the streets due to her Aryan appearance. If Silvia were forced to wear the yellow star, she would be subjected to the same public sneers and insults that had been previously directed only at me.

Occasionally, when we were together, a passerby would look at the cute little blond girl walking by my side, and mutter something about a good little German girl playing with a Judenschwein (Jew swine). After a while, I became quite used to being called by that epithet. I did ask Mutti how everyone knew I was Jewish. Was it my nose?

Mutti—bless her—convinced me that I had a noble Roman nose, and I would "grow into it". She tried to deal with my growing awareness about looking Jewish by also telling me about a continent called India where every girl looked like me. She said the women of India were considered very beautiful and graceful. She even located a book of poems by the Indian writer Rabindranath Tagore, and read them to me in the German translation. She also explained that the matriarchs in the Bible—Sara, Rebecca, Rachel, and Leah—must have looked like me. I secretly became quite satisfied with my appearance.

We left Germany just before the law was passed requiring Jews to wear the mandatory sign of Jewishness, the Star of David. Now, when I see that proud symbol of the State of Israel, and of my religion, I still have memories of the time when the Nazis tried to make this star a symbol of shame.

Chapter Twenty-Eight

Berlin 1939
Change is in the Air

One of my favorite childhood daydreams concerned the almost other-worldly Zeppelins that silently appeared from time to time in the sky over Charlottenburg.

My first glimpse of those graceful floating giants was when Hannah, Alexander and I were playing Marbles in the small park Olivaer Platz after school one day. Suddenly my friend Hannah looked up and let out a yell. There, hovering silently almost directly above us, was a huge, silver colored, cigar-shaped apparition—a Zeppelin. I knew immediately what it was. Papa had shown me a photograph in the newspaper that pictured this flying machine. It glided silently and then just hung, gently swaying in place, reflecting the sunlight and looking like something from a fairytale.

Alexander said that there were people in the little cabin that was stuck to the bottom of the airship. We could see a row of windows glinting in the reflected sunlight. I was enchanted with this strange object hovering so low over the roofs of the apartment buildings and trees around us.

That evening my imagination took over when I again overheard my parents discuss their ongoing attempts to leave Berlin and Germany. In my daydream, I visualized our escape by Zeppelin. Maybe I could learn to toss a rope up to that little cabin, where a kindly person would open one of those windows, lean out and haul up the ladder I had tied to the other end.

Then Papa, Mutti, Silvia and I would quickly climb up this ladder, and the Zeppelin would soar high into the sky and silently float all the way over the ocean to America where Mutti's cousins would be waiting for us in a city called Newark. They would be assembled to watch us slide down a rope into their waiting arms.

This fantasy, which I never told to anyone, became my vehicle for temporarily escaping the constant fear of that "Knock at the door at 2 a.m." and I watched for these friendly giants to appear so magically in the sky over Niebuhr Strasse.

Now, whenever I see pictures of U.F.O.s, they instantly and vividly remind me of my childish hopes. I still recall my image of a "Knight In Shining Armor"—the huge silver-gray Zeppelin glittering in the sunlight—that would float silently high over our apartment building in Charlottenburg—having come to rescue me and my family and take us far away from the prevailing terror in the streets of our city.

On my way home from school one afternoon, I happened to pass the window of a large furniture store on the Tauentzin Strasse. I was then attending the hastily organized Jewish High School on Wilsnacker Strasse that had been created by the Jewish education authorities in Berlin. All of us students had been in Jewish schools located in different sections of Berlin. These were forcibly closed by the Nazis, and we were all in transition.

Mutti and Papa were desperately trying to locate any hospitable country in the world that would grant us entry visas. Most of us, including Silvia and me, had been registered on the Kindertransport list and were waiting to be told when to report for that fateful trip to England without our parents.

My curiosity was aroused when I came upon a crowd of people all intently staring into the display window. I eased my way forward and soon heard, then saw, what the attraction was. There stood a large furniture cabinet, about one meter high, nicely paneled with decorative woods, with a little glass window, faintly blue in color, in the front near the top. This small window was about seven centimeters wide by five centimeters high.

Visible on this tiny screen was Adolf Hitler, ranting and gesturing in his odd Austrian-accented German about his usual subject "eradicating the Jews to produce a pure Aryan Germany." The shop owners had rigged a loudspeaker, so we could hear, as well as see, this performance. I glanced around. Most of the people standing near me had their right arms stiffly raised in the 'Heil Hitler' salute and were nodding in agreement with their Fuehrer's shouting.

I felt like sinking into the ground. I turned around and ran home as fast as possible. This was the first time I saw a "FERNSEH-APPARAT" ("Far-Viewing-Machine") that was probably one of the first television sets in Europe. This contraption brought Hitler into the very streets that I walked. I was more frightened than ever, and shared my parents' overwhelming relief when the temporary visa from England arrived enabling our entire family to leave Berlin and get out of Germany. Within a day we finished packing, bought railway tickets to Hamburg, and hastily departed Berlin. Silvia and I had been firmly instructed by our parents not to say goodbye to our friends for fear of being stopped at the last minute. I was happy to leave behind the little Hitler on that tiny bluish screen threatening us with extinction.

Our next stop would be Hamburg, and then on to Grimsby, England.

Chapter Twenty-Nine

Berlin 1939
Grandma Rozanski

My middle name is Malkah in memory of my father's mother, Malkah Braverman Rozanski, who died several years before I was born. She and Opa Nissan were married in Bialystok, Russia around 1896. Papa, their oldest child, was born on July 8, 1897. She was an orthodox woman, observing all the Jewish laws and traditions and keeping a kosher home. She also did not want to be photographed for frivolous reasons. In all her life, she was probably photographed twice. I have one photo of her with Opa. She's wearing a stiff, obviously heavy ritual wig—a Sheitel—I think it must have been their wedding photo.

The other photograph is on an official identity card, with German writing, and was taken during the German occupation of Bialystok in World War One, when every resident had to carry such a document. This photo shows she was already quite ill. Her hair is pulled pack severely from her face and she was wearing a plain, dark shift.

Papa told me food was very scarce during the occupation, and she regularly sent him to the German Army barracks to ask the army cook for the potato peels he usually threw out. Papa also collected any bits of vegetables he could find in the garbage bin. My Oma cooked this into a soup to feed her husband and seven children. She had a hard life. It showed in the lines on her face in the tiny identity photo my father treasured.

While we were living in Berlin, in the chaos of the Nazi-generated rules against Jews and dissenters, my father was approached by a well-known German portrait painter, Herr von Riebe. This artist, who was not Jewish, had made statements in public about his sentiments regarding the Nazi persecution of his Jewish friends. For making these statements, he received the dreaded notice about having to be ready on a certain date for transfer to a concentration camp that specialized in "reforming" political dissidents.

He asked my father, who still had his contracting business, to give him a job as house painter under an assumed name. Papa immediately hired him, and at great risk employed him till Herr von Riebe could get a Visa for Argentina. When it was almost time for the artist to leave Berlin, he asked Papa how he could express his gratitude at being sheltered and employed while hiding from the Nazis. Papa showed him the tiny identity photo he had of his mother. Herr von Riebe took it to his studio and painted a wonderful, life-size portrait of my Oma.

We hid this painting in our luggage when we escaped from Berlin. It now hangs on my living room wall. I remember Papa telling me that it was so lifelike, it was as though his mother had posed for the artist. The painting shows a very weary, obviously suffering woman—with sad eyes. I think she must have known how sick she was.

She looks so old and tired I have to remind myself that she was only in her forties at the time of her death. When Papa took me on that trip to Bialystok, he went to visit her grave and say Kaddish—together with his sister, my Tante Taibah. Unfortunately, I never knew either of my grandmothers. I have always considered this such a lack in my life.

Chapter Thirty

August 1939
Berlin to Hamburg to England

"Sit on the suitcases, and wait for us," were my parents' instructions as they left Silvia and me alone on a long stone pier jutting into Hamburg harbor. Early that morning we had packed those suitcases in Berlin, rushed for the train to Hamburg, and taken a taxi to the harbor.

The last few weeks in Berlin had been filled with frantic attempts by my parents to obtain a Transit-Visa from the British Embassy, which would enable us to enter England as 'Friendly Aliens' and be allowed to stay just six weeks. Then we would have to leave, or be forced to leave, to return to Germany. A return to Germany was to be feared because a transportation order to a concentration camp had been delivered to us by mail.

We were issued this Visa because we already had a Visa for the United States, but our high Quota number would not come up for several months. We knew that war was imminent, and getting out of Germany would then be impossible. This temporary British Transit-Visa arrived in the same mail as the final notice from the French Embassy refusing to grant us permission to enter France as refugees.I remember Mutti's tears and Papa's clenched fists after first opening the letter from France—and then their almost hysterical laughter of relief when they opened the envelope from England, granting us a six-week haven, if we could find transportation.

So here we were in Hamburg, Silvia and I sitting on our suitcases on this long, unfriendly, deserted pier. It was late afternoon and would soon be getting dark. I knew I was responsible for the safety of my ten-year-old sister. I worried about what I could do if my parents failed to return. After all, they looked Jewish and were running from ship to ship looking for a space on any vessel that would take us to England, Scotland, Ireland or Wales. This frantic searching would make them look suspicious to any Nazi in the vicinity.

The wait was an eternity to me. To think that I might soon have to decide what to do about my sister and me if my parents failed to return upset me. To my great relief I never had to make that decision because after about an hour I heard my name called. I saw my parents running towards us, smiling and waving some papers.

They had persuaded the captain of a British fishing trawler to give us space on his ship. Named the **H.M.S. Bury**, it was leaving in a few hours for the fishing port of Grimsby on the east coast of England north of London. We literally pushed ourselves into the tiny, two-bunk cabin allotted to us. I had never experienced such relief in my entire life. I recall a very choppy sea on the overnight trip with us in our street clothes and crammed into the bunks.

Normally Silvia and I would have pushed each other to maneuver for more space, but this night we slept peacefully on that little ship. It was our first night of freedom from the threat of arrest and deportation. The war began September 3, 1939. Our six-week visa was extended indefinitely. Now we could never be forced to return to Germany nor to the threat of a concentration camp.

Chapter Thirty-One

Safe in England 1939
Grimsby to London to Braunston

Our arrival on the **H.M.S. Bury** at Grimsby is lost in the mist of time in my memory. I vaguely recall our being met by a representative of a Refugee organization, who must have been notified by Papa via telegram before we boarded the small fishing trawler in Hamburg. This man escorted us to a train station, and probably contacted the Hochbergs in London to come and meet us at the vast station in London— where we arrived, still seasick and exhausted, but jubilant and giddy with relief to be in the country that had offered us a six-week safe haven from Nazi persecution.

The Hochbergs were friends of friends, and had offered to put us up for a few days till we could find lodging in London. They did come to the station and took us to their very small, suburban house in the Cricklewood section of London. We were given a small room with two single beds and managed to stay there about a week before everyone's patience wore thin.

My father located two small rooms in a walkup tenement building. There were about six rooms opening onto each stair landing, with total strangers sharing the use of one toilet cubicle and one sink. Still we were suddenly free of the constant dread of arrest and shipment to a concentration camp. All of us felt such vast relief that we were smiling most of the time. I had not realized how tense and grim my parents were those last few months in Berlin. With very limited funds, we bought a small, second-hand card table, four folding chairs, and a used box spring and mattress. The mattress was placed on the floor in one room for my parents to sleep on. The box spring was put on the floor in the second room, to be shared by Silvia and me. After the first night on these old bed parts, all of us woke up bitten all over our bodies by bedbugs—a unique and disgusting experience.

My parents registered at Bloomsbury House, the central information-and clearing-house for all Jewish refugees arriving in London. All practical help about managing in this new country came to us from this agency. We were told that Silvia and I had to be enrolled immediately in a neighborhood school, so we could be evacuated from the City of London as a precaution against the coming war with Germany.

We did not speak or understand any English, except the inane phrases we had learned in our attempt to prepare ourselves while still in Berlin. Every morning, Silvia and I trouped off to the Geneva House School for Girls, on Kilburn High Road. Evenings we returned to the two rooms we now called home. Often other refugees visited us who had just arrived in London. If they didn't have a place to stay, my parents gladly shared our box-spring and mattress setup with these grateful refugee friends and acquaintances from Berlin. Most nights Silvia and I had to share our box-spring by lying across it, so there was room for at least two more people to lie down.

Every evening we gathered around our little card table. Papa conducted "English lessons" by reading out loud from the evening papers. We all tried to make sense of this new language and my parents also went to language classes arranged by Bloomsbury House. One morning, as Silvia and I entered our school, we were directed to board a bus that was waiting outside. Both of us suddenly realized that we might never see our parents again, and had not even been able to say a proper goodbye. After a long trip, by bus, train, and bus again, we arrived in the village of Braunston in Northamptonshire. Some kind and very gentle women from a local volunteer group parcelled us out to those residents of Braunston who had agreed to accept evacuated children into their homes.

We were taken, exhausted and very frightened, to the village home of Mr. and Mrs. Overton. We did not realize till much later how fortunate we were. These kind-hearted and loving people somehow managed to communicate their great good will to us and made us feel safe and secure.

Chapter Thirty-Two

Braunston 1939
Mr. & Mrs. Overton

The village of Braunston lies at the junction of two major canal systems in Northamptonshire, the Grand Union canal, and the Oxford canal. We were later taught in the village school that most canals in Great Britain originated as drainage ditches dug by the capable engineers of the Roman Army of Occupation of the country of "Britannica" many hundreds of years ago.

During World War II, the canals were the commercial arteries of England. The long narrow barges carried fuel, war supplies and food from one end of the country to the other. Since fuel for the large lorries (trucks) was rationed and in very short supply, the canal barges were the preferred method of transporting goods and supplies from city to city because the barges were pulled by horses walking along the tow paths next to the waterways. Braunston residents were very proud to point out to us evacuees the lovely little cast-iron bridge that spanned the canal. It was the only one of its kind in the country. We also heard of the 280 yard long tunnel that carried the canal under and through a local mountain.

When Silvia and I were brought to the door of the home where the Overtons lived, we did not realize how lucky we were. Mr. and Mrs. Overton literally welcomed us with open arms. It was late in the evening of August 30, 1939. Silvia and I were confused and frightened. We had no idea where we were. When we got off the bus at the Village Green, there were women volunteers from the local Ladies' Guild to "distribute" us among those Braunston residents who had been willing to accept London evacuees into their homes.

The Overtons soon learned that we did not understand a word they were saying, so Mrs. Overton decided to give us a big hug of welcome, clasping us to her ample, soft bosom, and then set about making us some hot cocoa, and toast with Lemon-Curd. This was a strange but delicious food for us. There was no electric toaster. The toast was made by impaling a slice of bread on the tines of a very long-handled fork and then holding this up to the blazing coal fire in the cast-iron kitchen stove. Even now, when I spread Lemon Curd on my toast, I am reminded of the warmth of welcome we received in that small Overton cottage.

We were taken upstairs to the bedroom that we were going to share with Phyllis, the Overton's teenage daughter. All of us slept in one large bed with hot water bottles snuggled at our feet. Phyllis sat up in bed to say her prayers. We had no idea what she was doing, having always been taught to pray to God in Hebrew. We thought that was the only language God understood.

Mrs. Overton had a lot of patience with our stumbling and stuttering attempts to learn English. She quickly asked us to call her "Mum" and to address her husband as "Dad". We had been accustomed, as long as we could remember, to be reviled by Christian people, and called names like "Judenschweine". Certainly we had never been treated with kindness and respect. Mum was very caring and concerned with everyone in the village who might need her help or compassion. She particularly kept an eye on Auntie Kate, our next door neighbor, a tiny slim woman who was the village laundress.

Dad was a folk artist, employed by the Braunston Shipyards at the canal, and his specialty was to hand-paint the colorful roses and castles on the tinware that was used by the "Bargies" to decorate their tiny cabins at the stern of the long canal barges. They were regarded like gypsies, having no home other than the tiny cabins in which they lived, cooked, and had their babies. They seemed content with their lives. Their school-age children were billeted with village residents during the semesters. When they reached the age of fourteen, they were put to work on the barges to help their families with the tedious hard work of navigating the narrow canals and the many locks that were part of their daily workday.

Dad explained to us the tradition behind the roses that he painted so deftly. He called them Tudor Roses and they showed his love for all flowers. His passion was for growing flowers in his garden. He raised Sweetpeas, those fragrant, pastel colored flowers that looked like little Orchids to me. He also grew huge richly colored Dahlias because they were Mum's favorite flowers. During the growing season, Dad picked a bouquet for Mum every day to put on her kitchen table.

On the outskirts of the village he farmed a patch of ground called an "allotment". Here he grew potatoes and other vegetables. Most villagers also grew their own produce. This generated much swapping of vegetables between families every day.

The milkman came by every day with his horse-drawn wagon. He had the milk in huge stainless steel milk cans, and ladled out the still warm, fresh milk that came from his own cows, into the pitcher that Silvia or I took out to the street for him to fill. He also sold freshly churned butter and homemade cheeses. All this required not only money, but a certain number of ration coupons, which complicated his life no end. The bread man also passed the house every day with big, crusty loaves of "Cottage Bread". This was a small loaf on top of a big loaf baked together. The egg-woman, who owned a flock of chickens, called every week lugging her basket of fresh brown eggs carefully protected from breakage by a nest of torn bits of newspaper. Mum saved the *Daily Mirror* for this woman and gave her a stack of them when she called at the Overtons cottage each week.

Dad used to take Silvia and me for walks around Braunston, where he'd point out various buildings of interest including the Braunston Village church. Silvia and I had never been inside a church, so we were very curious and asked many questions about everything we saw inside that ancient building.

This was the first time I realized how friendly Christians could be to Jews. Dad and Mum were simple, unpretentious people who showed us real hospitality and offered us love and safety. We were the first Jews they had ever met. They were a revelation to us, having grown up with the hostility and threats of the Nazi regime in Berlin. Here we were experiencing unconditional love and caring. Dad helped us to learn English by pointing to an object, saying its name, and then having us repeat it until he was sure we understood the meaning of the word and were able to pronounce it without a German accent.

When I had learned enough English to have meaningful conversations with Dad, he told me that he was sure our parents would survive the war and the bombings in London, and that we would all go off to America as my parents had planned. He predicted that I would return some day, drive up to the Overton home in a fancy American car, and we'd sit and talk about 'old times".

I did return to Braunston in 1969, with my husband Kenneth and our teenaged son, but Dad and Mum had long since died. I returned again for the funeral of Phyllis who had died of cancer. When I stood in the Braunston churchyard at their three graves, I gave silent thanks to these wonderful people for taking Silvia and me into their home, for taking care of us, and demonstrating to us that there are good people in this world. Instead of hating and reviling us for our religion, they shared with us a safe life and a happy family.

Chapter Thirty-Three

Braunston 1939/1940
Learning Improper English

After settling in at the Overtons, we were enrolled in the Braunston Village School. The first few days at school went by in a bewildering haze of listening to our teachers and fellow pupils and understanding very little of what we heard.

My lack of understanding was noted with great pleasure by Hector Wilson, the "bad boy" of the village. He was older than the other children in our class and had been held back several times instead of being promoted to the next grade. After about two weeks, when I was sporadically beginning to comprehend my fellow students, he approached me in the school yard during recess sporting a big smile, and said, "You learn English song."

He took me to one side, where nobody could hear him, and started singing to teach me a song composed mostly of four-letter words that I didn't understand. He patiently sang the song over and over, and made me repeat his words and melody till he was satisfied that I remembered them. Then he told me to sing it for Mrs. Overton, as a big surprise because, he said, she would be so happy that I was learning an old English folk song.

After school that afternoon, on the way home, I tried to teach it to Silvia, who was a very quick study. By the time we entered Mrs. Overton's kitchen, we were ready to surprise her with Hector's song. Of course we had no idea what we were singing.

Mrs. Overton gasped and blushed, then tried to hide a smile when she asked who had taught us this song. I told her, in my limited English, that Hector had been very kind to take the time to teach it to us. She walked up the street to Hector's home where he lived with his parents. I heard the next day that his father gave him a good hiding.

Occasionally, even now, the words and melody come to mind. And I have to smile to think how clever Hector was in playing this prank. I have been told that he now lives in the States, and is an executive in a large corporation.

Chapter Thirty-Four

Braunston 1940
Gas Masks and Disaster Drills

My most important possession was my Government Issue gas mask. Such a rubbery-smelling device had been given to every resident of Great Britain in the chaotic days before the beginning of WW-II. The rule was that nobody was to be seen in public without the little cardboard carton, containing the mask, hanging around their neck.

A new industry quickly developed. It produced containers and covers that made the masks look like fashion accessories. We immigrants could not afford such frippery and wore the plain brown boxes hanging on a black string wherever we went. Of course we had to bring them to school in Braunston and official school rules decreed that we have a "Gas Mask Drill" three times a week. When the school bell rang, we all had to don our masks and dive under our desks, crouching there till the "All Clear" bell sounded.

What made this interesting was that Hector, who today would be called a Class Clown, soon discovered that by inhaling large, gasping breaths, he was able to make his gas mask assume weird expressions, reducing us all to helpless laughter. This also caused sensitive Trevor to start heaving and gagging, which usually brought on a fit of vomiting for this boy. Soon the whole class would react to the smell of vomit and rip off their masks. This pleased Hector no end. His fun was quickly thwarted as the teachers soon learned to send Hector outside whenever the alarm sounded to practice his gas mask drill in isolation.

A more enjoyable Emergency Drill involved all of us children learning how to administer First Aid in case the village of Braunston was bombed by the Luftwaffe. Our teacher carried a basket around the room with little folded pieces of paper in it, and asked half the class members to pick one. Each paper had written on it a different injury. The student then had to simulate the injury that had been indicated on the paper, such as broken leg, head wound, spinal injury, spitting blood, and paralysis. In good weather we did this on the Village Green, much to the amusement of passers-by.

Those students without an injury designation had to practice First Aid on the "unfortunate wounded". We were taught how to set a broken bone, how to apply a tourniquet, how to improvise a stretcher, and how to revive someone who wasn't breathing. Naturally, Hector always wanted to practice mouth-to-mouth resuscitation on the prettiest girls.

We were supplied with torn sheets to use as bandages, and red ink to simulate bleeding. We were given splints; tying up our fellow students to these rough wooden planks was a real thrill, particularly when they loudly complained that the bandages were too tight.

Members of the local Women's Club were often present at these drills to serve, in enamel mugs, strong, sweet, but lukewarm tea to all the 'casualties'. All of us enjoyed these drills immensely. They were great fun despite the seriousness of what these exercises represented. And they were a welcome break from chanting the arithmetic tables: "One and One are Two, Two and Two are Four, Three and Three are Six," and so on. Even today, I can hear that droning chant whenever I balance my checkbook.

Chapter Thirty-Five

Braunston 1940
Mr. & Mrs. Turner

The local post office in Braunston consisted of a small counter in a grocery store run by Mr. and Mrs. Turner. This couple, along with the Overtons and Auntie Kate, deserve my eternal gratitude. When I arrived in their village, I was suspicious and frightened of anyone who wasn't Jewish. In my thirteen years I had experienced much persecution and cruelty at the hands of non-Jews and had learned to keep my distance and not to trust anyone of a different religion.

The Turners were like most of the people we met in Braunston, gentle, friendly, and welcoming to us little "aliens" who didn't speak English and had very different manners from the inhabitants of Braunston, near Rugby, Northamptonshire.

Mr. Turner was a genial, middle-aged man who, with his wife, ran the grocery store and the little post office. He took a particular liking to Silvia and me. He and his wife became our surrogate family, along with the Overtons with whom we lived. Every Sunday afternoon Silvia and I were invited to

Tea at the Turners in their home on the upper two floors over their store.

With rationing in effect, the food at the Overtons was plentiful but very plain. The exciting snacks and treats served at the Turners' Teas were the high point of our week. Mrs. Turner, with great patience, also started to teach us English. She insisted that we speak no German in her house, and soon Silvia and I were able to converse, on a basic level, with each other in English.

As soon as our schoolmate Hector found out about our weekly invitations to the Turners, he decided to be "helpful" and offered to teach us the names of English foods that would be served at teatime in the Turner home. He told us that a special delicacy was something called "Toe-Jam". He suggested we surprise the Turners by asking for it, to put on our scones. When I hesitatingly mentioned Toe-Jam, Mr. Turner burst out laughing. Winking at his wife, he explained to us what Toe-Jam really was; something disgusting connected with unwashed feet. I was appalled and embarrassed. But Mrs. Turner immediately surmised that we had learned this expression from Hector, whom she knew to be a practical joker. She calmed me down and suggested that we should not to learn any more English words or songs from our schoolmate.

After tea, the Turners brought out the Sunday newspaper and had Silvia and me read out loud. They then had us explain what we were reading to be sure that we understood the news about the war. They wrote letters to my parents in London, assuring them that we were well looked after, and promising to keep an eye on us.

When I visited Braunston in 1969, the Turners were retired and living in a modern house near the Braunston church. Their son was running the business with his wife and living over the store. Mr. Turner was quite ill, but as sweet and kind as ever. He asked about my sister, and wondered if he ever would see little Silvia again. When I told her about this, she immediately made reservations and flew to England, to visit the Turners and talk about the times when Mr. Turner had given her rides on the handlebars of his bicycle as he delivered the "Post". He died soon after her visit.

Mrs. Turner, however, lived past her hundredth birthday, in a nursing home near Braunston. She and I corresponded regularly until she was in her late nineties. I helped her with her hobby of tatting lace by sending her samples whenever I found pieces of this lace in antiques stores.

I consider myself very fortunate to have known these wonderful, generous and loving people. They totally changed my attitude and feelings about having to be cautious and frightened around non-Jews. It was just plain good luck that Silvia and I were sent to Braunston during the war. It was the ideal refuge for us, and we got to know, love, and trust the English people we met there.

Chapter Thirty-Six

Braunston 1940
Auntie Kate

Papa used to tell me that there's a special place in heaven that is reserved for those who please God while on this earth; those who are selfless and do good deeds and ask nothing for themselves. If I'm lucky enough to go to that higher region when I die, and if I'm allowed a glimpse into that special area that my father told me about, I know I will see Auntie Kate sitting on a little bench at the feet of God surrounded by legions of her beloved kitty cats that were her "family" when I knew her in Braunston.

Miss Kate Danks—or Auntie Kate, as everyone in the village called her—was the Overtons' next door neighbor. She was incredibly small—probably under 5 feet tall and very, very thin. She wore layers of old, shapeless, ripped clothing, at least four pairs of socks on top of one other, and ankle boots for all the walking she had to do. She was the village laundress. Auntie Kate walked a weekly route to customers to collect the shirts that had been worn, took them home and hand-washed and ironed them. She then walked these same miles again, delivering the crisp, white folded shirts that had been through her care. She never married, and lived with fourteen cats that she adored.

She spent most of the money she earned from her laundry work at Hargave the Butcher buying mincemeat and beef-liver with her precious food-ration coupons, to make sure her kitties got the best meals. Auntie Kate herself existed mostly on slices of bread and margarine, endless cups of strong tea, and the dinners Mum prepared for her that I was designated to bring to Auntie Kate's kitchen door several times a week. I was given strict orders by Mum to sit down and watch Auntie Kate actually eat the meal because otherwise she'd give most of it to her cats. At Auntie Kate's request, I was also allowed to sleep in her cottage because she was sure the Luftwaffe would bomb Braunston. After all, it was on the Grand Union canal and a perfect target for Hitler's bombers!

She felt safer with me around. I loved spending time listening to her tell stories about her life as a young woman. Her father had been a railroad man who performed maintenance on the big steam engines in the Railroad Maintenance Yards of Rugby.

Auntie Kate must have been present at many home births in the village because, as a young woman, she assisted the local midwife. She confounded me with tales of babies born with "veils" over their faces, which with my still limited English, I assumed to be bridal veils. My mental image of those babies was very picturesque. Toothless Auntie Kate could have used the money she earned from her laundry work to purchase a set of false teeth, which she so obviously needed, but the welfare of her many cats came first. Their care and feeding was what motivated Auntie.

Every evening, she prepared a cot in front of her fireplace for me while she slept in her easy chair. She wanted to be ready in case of an air raid to jump up, collect her cats, and put them all in the cubby hole under the stairs, which was supposed to be the safest place in any house. Sometimes, when I cried myself to sleep, I'd feel her gently stroking my hair and comforting me by saying, "There, there, my darling. It will all be all right soon."

Auntie Kate was a true and pure human being. She never thought about her own needs. When she did have a few shillings to spare, she bought some extra bread and jam, filled a thermos with her strong tea, and took Silvia and me on a picnic in the fields around Braunston. We'd pick blackberries in the brambles that formed the hedges around the fields. Mum would bake these shiny, fragrant berries into the most delicious pie, which was served with warm custard and our cocoa in the evenings.

My first close contact with any citizens of our new home country was with the Overtons and Auntie Kate. These three people totally loved and protected Silvia and me. For the first time in our lives we were able to form strong bonds of trust and affection with people who were not Jewish. This was a miracle to me. I often wondered what would happen to my little sister and me if our parents were hurt or killed in the steady bombing that London was experiencing. We listened to the B.B.C broadcasts about the war every evening and I felt that at the very least, Silvia and I would have a loving home if we had nobody to go back to when the war ended.

My parents wrote to us regularly, first in German, and after a few months in English, reminding us of the dates of Jewish Holidays. The Overtons and Auntie Kate encouraged us to celebrate our festivals as best we could. Mum baked a special cake for us, and Auntie Kate got us candles and opened a very old bottle of wine that one of her customers had given her some years ago. We did not realize, till much later, the incredible patience and kindness that these three people demonstrated when dealing with two strange little girls who could neither speak nor understand English, who cried a lot at night, and who were of a faith they had barely heard of.

During my return visit to Braunston with my family in 1969, I did walk up the long hill to Auntie's house. She was even smaller and thinner than I remembered. She seemed to be wearing the same colorless, patched clothes that I had seen her wear during the war. She was still completely toothless, but her smile was as warm as ever. She must have been almost a hundred years old, but continued taking wonderful care of her now eighteen kitties that were living with her at the time. As I did in the war days, I listened as she told me the names and histories of all her cats. Again I was reminded that I was in the presence of a rare and special human being.

After that trip, whenever my husband went to Europe on business, he'd stop at Harrods in London, to order a large food parcel to be shipped to Auntie Kate. I always reminded him to send "people food" like canned fruit, vegetable soups and packages of rice and spaghetti. Otherwise I knew everything would end up in the cats' food bowls. Auntie Kate and I kept up a correspondence that on her part consisted mostly of news about her cats and her neighbors in that order. She also offered occasional corrections of my English spelling and grammar, as she used to do when I was living in Braunston. One time she wrote that I had obviously not yet finished learning English!

When a note came from a niece of hers, telling me that Auntie had died in her sleep, surrounded by her feline family, I felt that I had lost a precious friend. Auntie Kate, Dad and Mum were my introduction to a non-Jewish world that, as a little girl, I barely knew existed.

Chapter Thirty-Seven

London 1940
Earning an Income

Within a week of my parents getting settled in their bug-infested rooms, it had become obvious to them that the small amount of money we had been permitted to take out of Germany was not going to last long in London.

Fortunately, before we left Berlin in such a hurry, Papa had obtained an International Drivers' License. With this license in his possession, he was able to obtain a job as a truck driver in London even though he barely understood English, didn't know the streets of the city, and had to drive on the left. Even with these hindrances he managed to earn a weekly wage.

This income was supplemented by Mutti's sewing, using her treasured sewing machine that Herr Foerster had so graciously permitted her to keep and bring to London. She contacted a fellow refugee from Berlin, Herr Kaiser, who had arrived the year before and opened a successful dress manufacturing business. He kept Mutti busy with large bundles of partially sewn dresses, into which Mutti had to insert zippers, and then hand-sew the hems. She was pleased that she was able to supplement the family income with her skilled hands.

When I returned from Braunston, I became her Delivery Person—at 14 years of age. I'd take a bus to Cavendish Square, to pick up and deliver her work to the Kaiser workroom. This often became a real adventure because of the frequent and sudden air raid warnings, followed by the Ack-Ack guns placed in all the London parks, and the loud whine of the descending bombs. When this happened, I had to get off the bus, run into an air raid shelter, and sit with my bundles of dresses to wait for the All-Clear sirens to sound.

In my third year at Willesden College, I had Fridays off, so Herr Kaiser offered me a job in his workroom designing and making patterns for dresses. I also sketched the finished garments for his sales catalog. This was the foundation of my career as a fashion designer.

Chapter Thirty-Eight

London 1941
Robert

My parents' close friends from Berlin, the Manheims, lived near us in London. One day Papa came back from a visit to the Manheims, very upset. He told us that the Manheims' nephew Robert had been there to visit his uncle and aunt. Robert was living in one of the hostels which had been organized in haste to provide shelter for the children arriving in England on the Kindertransports from Germany.

Robert, who was ten years old when his parents put him on that train, was very homesick and unhappy living in the hostel. It was overcrowded, and there was never enough food for all the children. By then he was twelve years old. He visited his uncle and aunt—his father's brother and his wife—every weekend. On one of these visits, Papa witnessed a scene that bothered him very much.

When it was time for Robert to return to his hostel, he started to cry and told his uncle that he did not want to leave. He pleaded to be allowed to stay with his uncle and aunt, but both Mannheims insisted that Robert had to go. Mr. Manheim said to my father, "We have enough problems taking care of our own sons. We can't cope with another boy."

Robert actually fell to his knees and embraced his uncle's legs, sobbing and promising not to be any trouble at all. Despite his tears and his pleading, his uncle and aunt remained adamant that he could not stay with them. Robert had to put on his coat and take the Underground train back to the hostel.

He felt so rejected by his family in London, that as soon as the war ended and he learned that his parents had perished in Auschwitz, he emigrated to Canada. He and his wife now live in Toronto. I am in touch with him via the Internet, and we have remained good friends.

Chapter Thirty-Nine

London 1941
Oh Baby!

When my parents got settled in London, they soon contacted former friends from Berlin. An active social life evolved. These friends entertained in each others' small flats, or even single rooms called "Bed-sitters". At such gatherings guests brought and shared whatever could be spared of their rationed biscuits, chocolate, or tea. Occasionally, someone brought coffee beans, a very desirable rarity. These beans were much appreciated by the host and were carefully hand-ground in a treasured old coffee mill from Germany. The ground beans were brewed and served with ceremony. Coffee was not always available even if one had the ration stamps for it. So serving coffee usually was the high point of a social afternoon.

Many topics of general interest were discussed. Often advice was offered on how to maneuver the complicated ins-and-outs of Bloomsbury House. This was the big clearing house set up by the Government to help refugees who were clueless about English laws and customs. Bloomsbury House also helped us to locate each other in London.

One young couple, Horst and Leonore, were regulars. They had known each other in Berlin, met again in London, and were newlyweds. Soon they announced with great joy that Leonore was pregnant. They told all of us that since their child would be born in England, and automatically be a citizen, the baby would not hear any German spoken. They had decided to speak only English in their home to make sure the child would not grow up in England speaking a foreign language. Eventually we heard the good news that a little girl had been born and given the very British name of Jane. We were kept informed, from time to time, about Jane's progress. The parents were proud that she was starting to speak, and in fluent English at that. Soon we were told we would all get to see and hear this Wunderkind—a child of two Germans parents who now spoke only English.

That day came, at an afternoon coffee hour, when two-year-old Jane was finally "unveiled". She was a pretty little girl though quite shy. After a while, Jane came over to the table, pulled at her mother's sleeve, and started to speak in her high clear voice, *"Mummy, pliss giff me dze boll. I vant to pley viz dze bollie. Vere iss my boll?"*

This lovely little English-born girl had heard only English spoken in her home, but, regrettably, it was the heavily German-accented English of both her parents. The proud smiles on her parents' faces prevented us from voicing anything but compliments about the fluency of their child's English. My parents and I avoided looking at one another. We knew that if we did we'd burst out laughing. But there were amused smiles all around.

We lost touch with Horst, Leonore and Jane when our family emigrated to the States, but I sometimes think of little Jane. I hope that she learned to shed the burden of that very heavy accent before she started school.

Chapter Forty

London 1941
Miss Gottfeldt

Charlotte Gottfeldt was a strikingly beautiful young woman. If I had to compare her with a well-known actress, I would say she looked much like Ava Gardner. She was the designer and pattern maker at Mr. Kaiser's fashion business. I was hired to work there part time to learn the business and to be Miss Gottfeldt's assistant.

When I first saw her, I thought I knew her. We soon established that she had been the Art and Sewing teacher in Silvia's school, the Hebrew Day School at the Fasanenstrasse Synagogue. I had met her in Berlin at a school function, which I attended with my parents and Silvia.

The other girls working at Herr Kaiser's business all addressed her as 'Lottie'. I could not bring myself to call her anything but 'Miss Gottfeldt". She was a patient teacher and readily admitted her mistakes when I corrected errors in patterns she drafted—I was studying pattern making at Willesden School of Art—and she and I became fast friends.

She confided to me that about a week before she fled Berlin she and her fiance went to a Rabbi and, with just their families in attendance, were married in his study. Her husband's papers to emigrate needed more work, so he had urged her to leave for London, promising he'd soon join her. Then the war started. He told her in his last letter to her from Berlin, which was hand-delivered to her by mutual friends who had escaped just in time, that he was about to be sent to Auschwitz. He wrote that he would survive and promised to join her after the war.

I so enjoyed working with Miss Gottfeldt. She was an optimistic young woman, and great company in my working life. One day, when I was out with friends walking on Oxford Street, I saw her arm-in-arm with a very handsome, well-dressed man, laughing and gazing at him with obvious affection. When she saw me, she looked away. I realized she did not want to be seen and certainly did not want to introduce her companion to me.

On our next working day, she saw how upset I was with her. After all, she had a husband in a concentration camp and she had promised to wait for him! She took me out to lunch and said to me, "You are very young—still a teenager. I don't expect you to understand, but when you're older, you will. I do love my husband, but I am here all by myself in England, and this is a different kind of relationship." She helped me realize that there are many degrees of affection, and love. She simply did not want to be completely on her own and missed the companionship of a male friend in her private and social life.

A few weeks later, when I came in to work, the girls in the sewing-room suddenly became very quiet. I looked around, saw that Miss Gottfeldt was not in the Design Department and asked where she was. One of the girls told me that Lottie was in the hospital. She had been burned over almost her entire body.

She lived in a small "Bed-sitter" that had an open electric fire to heat the room. The weather was cold and damp, and she was wearing a long fleece robe that had brushed against the fire and burst into flames. By the time the neighbors heard her screams and rushed to her assistance, she was critically burned.

This happened on a Friday. I intended to visit her in the hospital the following day, but she died during the night. I attended her funeral and among the mourners was her friend with whom I'd seen her on Oxford Street. All I could do was shake his hand. He spoke to me briefly saying that it would be ironic if her husband survived, and came to London after the war looking for her.

This is a story without a conclusion. I don't know if Lottie's husband or parents survived the Holocaust. What I do know is that a beautiful, intelligent, and very talented young woman, who was a dear friend, had been deprived of her future by an agonizing death.

A few days after Lottie's funeral, a woman came to the Kaiser workroom and asked to see me. She was Lottie's sister and she told me she had been cleaning out the flat of Lottie's possessions. She remembered Lottie talking about me, and how much we enjoyed working together. The sister had gathered up Lottie's watercolor paints and paint brushes and put them in a black metal box that she gave to me. I still have this memento of a spirited woman—a dear friend—and an unforgettable loss.

Chapter Forty-One

London 1942
Art School

When my parents brought me back to London from Braunston in 1941, their purpose was to offer me more opportunities for an education than were then available in the crowded Braunston Village school that was overflowing with children evacuated from the London school system. Silvia refused to leave. She was not ready to give up the relative safety from the Blitzkrieg that Braunston offered.

An appointment was made and I was taken to the fabled "Bloomsbury House" in central London for evaluation, and to find a school that would help develop my talents for Arts and Crafts. My mother spoke to a very dour man behind a desk. He abruptly shoved a paper and pencil at me, and said, "Draw something." I became immediately aware that my future education depended on this moment. I nervously looked around for inspiration on what to draw. I spotted a glass inkwell on his desk and carefully sketched this object with as much shading and depth as I could manage.

When I handed him my paper, he smiled for the first time. He told my mother that I was so talented I would qualify for an annual stipend to enable me to attend the Willesden College, School of Art. My mother and I celebrated our mutual delight by splurging for Tea at a nearby Lyons Corner House restaurant. This school was different from others I'd attended. I had to order and wear the burgundy blazer that was the school uniform. The list of art supplies was a wonderful discovery for me. The watercolor paint boxes, the pencils and erasers, and numerous brushes, some with bamboo handles, were my treasures and a total joy. I looked forward to filling the large pads of sketching papers with my own creations. Life was suddenly full of promise despite the frequent bombing of London by the Luftwaffe.

I absolutely loved boarding the bus every day, proudly wearing my burgundy blazer with the golden crest of Willesden College embroidered on the pocket. I carried a large black portfolio filled with my art work. In a short time I outgrew the blazer. The tightness around the shoulders, and the sleeves that became too short, did not bother me at all. I was, at last, just a regular student. I no longer had to worry about demeaning racial insults regarding foreigners and Jews. I wore my blazer so proudly! I finally looked like everyone else and had even learned the language and spoke it fluently.

For the first time in my life I was not an outsider. The feeling was indescribable. It was here that I met Marcelle. We connected, became close friends and, as a bonus, her parents and my parents also became good friends. We visited back and forth between Marcelle's house and our apartment often.

Marcelle was very knowledgeable about Hollywood movies. She had been in London enjoying them, while I, in the village of Braunston where there was no cinema, had the only entertainment available—listening to the nightly news broadcasts on the B.B.C. Marcelle filled in the huge gaps in my knowledge concerning films by showing me her fan magazines and regularly attending movies with me.

Chapter Forty-Two

London 1941-1942
Quentin Crisp

At Willesden College School of Art Marcelle and I attended most of our classes together. One day, as we entered our Life Class, I was ahead of Marcelle and saw the back of a graceful nude model already seated on the elevated platform. She had long, fiery red hair and carefully manicured slender hands with brightly lacquered long scarlet nails. It was a pleasure to see such a beautiful model after having had so many elderly women and obese men posing for us. Because most able-bodied men and women were in either the Armed Forces or serving in the war effort, they were the only models available to pose. I turned to Marcelle and said, "Thank heavens we've got a young woman posing today".

She walked around me to see the model from the front, took one look, hurried back to where I was setting up my easel and whispered, "I don't think so!" I was curious and walked around our model to the front of the room where, to my astonishment, I saw that our model was a man. He was exquisitely made up with eye shadow, mascara, lipstick and long, painted nails. I had never in my life seen such a being. I did nothing but stare until I reminded myself that we were there to draw.

During this lesson, the air raid sirens sounded. Following the instructions we had all been given, the class filed out of the classroom and onto the school grounds where air raid shelters had been dug. These were long, narrow Quonset-hut-like buildings set underground and lit by single, dim electric bulbs. These buildings were always damp, bad smelling and sometimes mice could be seen scurrying about.

As Marcelle and I huddled with the other students on the splintery wooden benches lining the walls of our shelter, listening to the crack of anti-aircraft fire, and the occasional whine of a descending bomb, we saw Quentin Crisp, our model, wearing a flowery silk kimono. He was strutting, like a fashion model with one hand on his hip, between the two rows of frightened art students and casually smoking a cigarette in a 10-inch long holder. He was absolutely calm. He smiled at us and suddenly the fear we all felt about what was happening outside receded. We began to talk and joke till the All Clear sounded.

Years later, in the 1980s, I reconnected with Mr. Crisp. I had read in the New York Times that an unusual one-man-show was being presented in Greenwich Village, and from the accompanying photograph, recognized Quentin Crisp. Only now he was a lavender-haired, dignified senior citizen, touring the world lecturing about his life style and adventures when he had lived as a highly visible gay man in war-time London.

I phoned him at the Algonquin Hotel where he was staying and made an appointment for my husband and me to meet him for drinks at the famous Algonquin Bar. I brought with me the life drawing I had made during the war. Although I had merely intended to show it to him, he assumed I was presenting it to him and graciously accepted it.

We invited him to lunch the next day at Silvia's apartment. When we drove up to the hotel the next morning, we saw him emerge from the entrance wearing a dramatic, wide-brimmed black hat, a flowing black cape, and a floating lavender chiffon scarf draped around his neck. He wore the same makeup that had startled me so when I first saw him posing at Willesden College in London.

A faint floral scent wafted around him. He was the perfect guest—entertaining us with stories of his career, as a Civil Servant for the London County Council that hired him to pose for Life classes in the school system. This was a government job and eventually resulted in his writing a book titled *The Naked Civil Servant*. His best anecdotes concerned his posing for Life Class students while the Blitzkrieg raged and wave after wave of Nazi bombers attacked the city of London.

After lunch he asked our permission to remove his shoes because, he said, as a young man he had ruined his feet by forcing them into shoes that were several sizes too small. This fitted in with his vision of how he wanted to be perceived as a Gay man. It must have taken great courage for him to show himself in the streets of the Eastend of London wearing his distinctive, colorful clothing and makeup, but he knew even then who and what he was. Being beaten up regularly by street gangs of local hooligans, as he called them, was a small price to pay for the statement he made with his makeup and his flaming hennaed red hair.

His books describe his steadfastness of holding onto his principles and not pretending to be anyone other than who he was. He lived long enough to be thoroughly vindicated. He became an admired role model for young men and women who recognized his courage in never wavering from his proud self-image as an uninhibited and liberated man who happened to feel "different", and chose not to hide it.

Chapter Forty-Three

London 1944
Mutti's War Wounds

It was 1944. The war in Europe was still going on. Hitler attacked London with a new weapon: the Flying Bomb, also called The Doodle Bug in the newspapers. It was a small airplane loaded with high explosives and an automatic pilot set to guide it to the sky over London. After being launched from Germany or France, The Flying Bomb was over London in a few minutes. When the fuel ran out, the engine stopped, the plane stalled, and then crashed onto the streets of the capital and exploded.

There was no specific target-or purpose-other than to kill as many civilians as possible. The plane had a distinctive, rumbling sound, and those of us on the ground learned to listen for its engine to stop, count to eight, listen for the whining descent and the loud explosion. If we were still alive, it had missed us! Of course the Royal Air Force scrambled to try to shoot these monsters down before they reached London, but they were not always successful. When the air raid sirens sounded, there usually was enough time for us to run to a shelter and hope the Doodle Bug would pass overhead and keep going.

My parents, Silvia and I were allotted bunks in the cellar of our apartment building. We started to go there in the late evening with pillows and blankets to spend the nights in relative safety, and not have to rush to the cellar when the sirens sounded. When Papa was not on duty as an Air Raid Warden, he joined us there.

My mother was claustrophobic. She also didn't like the mice that occasionally scurried around the bunks at night. One night I awoke in my bunk after a particularly loud explosion, to my father's frantic voice, "Get up! Help me look for Mutti! She's not down here." Silvia and I followed as my father ran up the four flights of stairs two at a time to the top floor. In front of our apartment door stood my bewildered mother, swaying and holding on to the door post, her entire face covered in blood.

I immediately fainted. Silvia ran to a corner of the stair landing and threw up. I was later told that my father picked up my mother in his arms, and while running down the stairs carrying her, he shouted for our neighbors to go up and take care of Silvia and me. Still carrying my bleeding mother, my father ran to the nearest First Aid Post, a block away, only to be told to find help elsewhere. People much more seriously hurt than my mother were being brought in with missing limbs. Still carrying her, he ran to the next block, and finally obtained First Aid for her. Eventually an ambulance came and took her to a hospital.

This same Flying Bomb that wounded my mother was a direct hit on the Bet Chalutz, a youth hostel in the next block. This was the home of German and Austrian teenagers who had escaped to London with the Kindertransport in 1939. Five of my friends living there were killed, and many others seriously wounded. The next day, while my mother's face was being stitched up in the hospital, I attended a funeral with five coffins. All the young people who knew and supported each other in the absence of family were there. I remember thinking that this was one of the saddest days I would ever experience.

I imagined that after the war was over their surviving families from the concentration camps would arrive in London, looking for their children whom they had sent to safety in England. When I got home, I talked with my father at length about the meaning of "Schicksal"—Fate—and how God could let such things happen to good people. I could see no reason why Mutti was wounded the night before, and almost lost her left eye and was now suffering great pain in a hospital. I also wanted to know what Papa thought about the funeral I had attended that day. We talked about his brothers and sisters, and his little nephew being in the midst of the horrors of Jewish persecution by the Germans who now occupied Poland. I don't remember my father's explanations. I don't think he had any way of making the war sound acceptable or rational to me. By then I was almost 18 years old and simply could not understand the unbelievable events occurring around us.

Much later, when Mutti was recovering, she told us that, as usual, she had not been able to tolerate the restricted space and dampness of the cellar shelter, so she had gone upstairs to our apartment to sleep in her own bed. The explosion had loosened the ceiling plaster over her bed and a huge chunk had fallen directly on her face. For the rest of Mutti's life, one side of her face was partially paralyzed. The nerves and muscles as well as her teeth had been badly injured. As she aged, the damage became more obvious, but she had a loving husband, as well as two devoted daughters, Silvia and me, to tell her that we loved her and thought she was beautiful.

Chapter Forty-Four

London to New York 1948
An Ending and a Beginning

All through the war years in England, my family's ultimate goal had been to re-institute our emigration applications at the American Embassy in London. The United States beckoned, through Hollywood films, and from letters relatives in the U.S. kept sending. They wrote about the "Golden Land", so as soon as the war was over, my parents started the lengthy and complicated proceedings to get us admitted into the U.S.A.

Silvia and I, having been born in Berlin, qualified for the German Quota which meant a short list with a very brief waiting time. Our parents, on the other hand, with their Polish passports, had to be entered on a very long waiting list to emigrate. Papa and Mutti decided that Silvia and I would emigrate as soon as we could and they would follow later. After all, I was twenty-one and Silvia nineteen—old enough to be responsible for ourselves and each other.

We crossed a very stormy Atlantic Ocean on the **S.S. America** in February 1948 to arrive in an ice-filled New York harbor, the result of freezing temperatures and the biggest snowstorm to have ever hit the North American East Coast. In the dim winter morning light, we passed the regal Statue of Liberty adorned with a mantle of snow.

After disembarking and meeting our relatives, who had come to welcome us, we finally started our new life with much anticipation and excitement. At last we had arrived in the country that we'd dreamed about, talked about, and tried to reach for years. Our lives really began again.

I have been married, and widowed three times. For the first time in my life I am actually a citizen of the country in which I live. I am blessed with a son, a daughter-in-law, and the two large extended and loving families I "inherited" from two of my marriages. I enjoy wonderful friendships that I formed in this country and, of course, I delight in my "old" friends from my childhood in Berlin and London including my co-authors Daisy, Lisa and Marcelle. The four of us have a friendship that has endured most of our lives—and after all these years I can still happily say: *. . . and now we are Four!*

Ellen's
Photo
Album

Berlin
Czechoslovakia
Warsaw
Bialystok
London
Braunston

Chapter One.
'The Beginning"
Berlin 1938
Ellen in school.
Age seven.

Chapter Four.
Family Times
Berlin 1930's.
Silvia, Mutti,
Ellen and Papa,
strolling on
Kurfuerstendamm.

Chapter Five.
"Grandpa from
Palestine."
Opa and Tante
Lotte on their
Wedding Day.
Berlin 1933.

Chapter Five.
Opa and Tante Lotte.
Haifa, Palestine,
1937.

Chapter Seven.
"Journeys with Papa."
Ellen and Papa
visit Uncle Zalmen.
Warsaw, Poland.
1936.

Chapter Nine.
Aunt Shayndel
on a visit to Berlin,
from Bialystock, Poland
Circa 1937.

Chapter Seven.
"Journeys with Papa."
Spindlermuehle,
Czechoslovakia 1936.

Wintersports—
Carefree times
with Papa. Sledding.
Iceskating. Skiing.
Spindlermuehle, 1936.

Chapter Seven.
"Journeys with Papa."
Papa's Family. Ellen and cousin Melech in front.
Bialystok, Poland. 1936.

Chapter Seven.
"Journeys with Papa."
Papa's sisters—Ellen's aunts, Peshka,
Shayndel, Rochel and Tayba—at the grave
of their mother, Malkah Braverman
Rozanski. Bialystok, 1930.

Chapter Eight.
"Hundekehle"
Ellen's mother,
Ryvkah Koslow Rozanski
Berlin 1936.

Chapter Ten.
"The Concert"
Ellen's parents,
Ryvkah and Aron.
Berlin 1937.

Chapter Seventeen.
Herr Foerster's "Loot."
(Mutti in our living room)
Berlin 1938.

Chapter Twentynine.
"Grandma Rozanski"
World War I
Occupation of Poland.
Circa 1917
German Identity Card.

Chapter Twentynine.
Portrait of Ellen's
grandmother,
Malkah Rozanski.
Painted in Berlin, 1939,
by Von Riebe.
From her W.W.I.
Identity card.

Chapter Eighteen.
"Yellow Benches and
Chocolate Cake"
Daisy, Silvia and Ellen.
Tiergarten, Berlin 1938.

Chapter Eighteen.
Daisy and Ellen in school.
Fasanenstrasse.
Berlin 1938.

Chapter Eighteen. Class Photo. Fasanenstrasse school. Our teacher, Dr. Kurt Aaron, stands in the back of the room. Daisy and Ellen are front row center. Next to us are Margot Roessler and Anastasia Schwartzleder. Berlin, 1938 .

Chapter Thirtyseven. "Earning a Living." Mutti and Papa visiting Marcelle's parents. In the garden behind their house on Hendon Way in London— circa 1942.

SCHOOL REPORT FORM.

Braunston SCHOOL.

REPORT *for Session* September, 1939 to Xmas 1939

NAME *Ellen Rozanski* CLASS *Special* No. of Scholars in Class

REPORT ON	FIRST TERM Ending Christmas 1939		SECOND TERM Ending 193	THIRD TERM Ending 193
Position in Class ..				
Reading	10	Excellent		
Literature				
Composition	8	Good.		
Writing	9	V. Good		
Arithmetic or Mathematics ..	8	Good.		
Geography				
History				
English Spelling	9	Very Good		
Science, Nature-Study, or Gardening				
Drawing	10	Excellent		
Handwork				
General Intelligence				
General Neatness ..				
Progress				
FOR GIRLS ONLY.				
Needlework				
Domestic Science ..				
Cookery				
Conduct	Excellent.			
Attendances made ..				
No. of Times Absent				
No of Times Late ..				
No. of Lessons Lost				

As I could only examine her in a few subjects this report is necessarily incomplete but she is making excellent progress and I am particularly pleased with her rapid advance in English reading & spelling

SIGNATURES
Class Teacher
Head Teacher *Wm J. Gould.*
Parent or Guardian of Scholar

N.B.—SCHOOL REOPENS on Wednesday, the 3rd of January, 1940

ckM-sc-m-ii-34,146s.   E. J. ARNOLD & SON LTD., EDUCATIONAL PUBLISHERS, LEEDS, GLASGOW & BELFAST.

Chapter Thirtytwo. "Mr. and Mrs. Overton." Ellen's first English report card after five months in England. Mr. Gould, the Headmaster at Braunston school, wrote the comment.

Chapter Thirtytwo. Silvia, Mr. Overton with Peggy the dog, Mrs. Overton and Ellen—at the Overtons' cottage in Braunston, England, 1940.

Chapter Thirtytwo. Silvia and Ellen in front of the Braunston church. 1940.

Reunion in Berlin! Ellen and Lisa meet again, after sixtyone years. May, 2000. Berlin, Germany.

Chapter Fortyone. Marcelle and Ellen on holiday in England, 1946.

Chapter Thirtynine. Revisiting Braunston in 1968. From left: Mrs. Turner, Mr. Harold Turner, Ellen, Jack Cockbill (Phyllis's husband), Phyllis Overton Cockbill, and Ellen's son, Steven Stein, in front.

Epilogue

. . . and now we are still Four—four lifelong friends. We hope that someone—sometime will read this, and marvel how we were able to enjoy, in the Nazi-dominated Berlin of the 1930s, many of the usual childhood experiences despite the inescapable threats to our freedom and our family security. We made friendships, attended school, enjoyed birthday parties, went ice skating, and played Marbles in the neighborhood parks. We were aware at an early age that our parents were desperately trying to find a safe haven for us almost anywhere in the world.

So, here we are—Daisy in Israel, Marcelle in the Boston area, and Lisa and I in New York. I know that the four of us are among the lucky ones. So many of our friends remained trapped in the Nazi bureaucracy unable to escape to safety. I am now a grateful citizen of the United States. I hope these memoirs will show our families and friends just how miraculous our escapes were. These adventures of our childhood shaped us into who we are today.

After seeing how everything my parents treasured was stripped from them, I still regard all my possessions as temporary. I continue to appreciate the right to vote and to travel where and when I please. I am the proud mother of a son born in the United States who has never had to look over his shoulder and cringe while uniformed bullies reviled him for being a Jew. Yes—we are indeed lucky—and our friendships endure.

My gratitude to my friend Millar Guthrie, a college classmate of my husband Kenneth Stein and now a retired editor, who graciously and patiently—sometimes impatiently !—proofread and edited most of our work—and who gave freely of his advice, experience and wisdom. Many thanks to Steve and Consuelo, my son and daughter-in-law, for their support and encouragement. AND of course, my great thankfulness to Daisy, Lisa and Marcelle for being my friends for a lifetime—and now joining me with enthusiasm in this venture. Thank you all!

Ellen Rozanski Stein . New York . 2005

Marcelle Robinson

Biographical Note

Marcelle Schidkowski Robinson, here seen in a 1948 photograph, is using her ancestral name to honor her father and keep his family name alive. She holds a Phi Beta Kappa, Magna cum laude degree in History, and a master's degree in classical studies from Harvard University, where she won First Prize for her thesis. She has published papers in several academic journals, and a travel article in *The Boston Globe*. Her latest paper has just been published, and a book-length biography, researched in Europe and the United States, is forthcoming. She has worked 25 years as a production coordinator for one of Boston's leading Public Radio stations, traveled extensively, and is now translating scholarly German articles for a Harvard museum. She has two married sons and two granddaughters, and lives with her husband and cat in a suburb of Boston.

MARCELLE ROBINSON - CONTENTS

Prologue

I am truly happy to be part of this group, but there are some significant differences between my story and those of Daisy, Lisa, and Ellen. Daisy, whom I vaguely remember meeting in London, Lisa, whom I've only just met, and Ellen were classmates already in Berlin. Ellen and I only go back as far as wartime London, long after the four cover pictures were taken. Secondly, I suspect that my secular German upbringing as a virtually non-practicing but nonetheless conscious Jew also sets me apart. My somewhat bizarre and hopefully atypical home life (had I chosen to write about it) might well have constituted a third.

The last, and for me perhaps the most emotional difference is the fact that I have no stories of loss, suffering or Nazi persecution to tell. All my memories are of an insulated world in which I was barely touched by the horrific events beginning to take shape around me.

Finally, a note of thanks to Ellen for sending me on this marvelous archaeological dig. I had been absolutely convinced that the six or seven double-spaced pages I initially sent her contained everything I could possibly remember about my early years. How wrong can a person be? She promptly sent me back to the drawing board with the admonition that there were many more memories "waiting in the wings" for me to write up. And so there were. My paper has since grown to some 18 single spaced pages. The memories are still coming, and my list of pictures keeps getting longer and longer. But I must stop somewhere.

MSR
April 2005

From Grunewald to Golders Green
A Collection Of Random Memories

By Marcelle Schidkowski Robinson

Part One: Memories of Berlin

Introduction

I was 11 years old in early 1938, when we left Berlin. Thanks to Good Fortune and my mother's astuteness and courage, we were among the lucky ones who escaped the Holocaust. And thanks to my indomitable aunt—my mother's sister, of whom more later—we even kept most of our belongings.

My family—for all intents and purposes, my entire family—consisted of my parents and my aunt. There were other family members, of course, but I had little or nothing to do with them, or they with me.

I was an only child, born 15 years into my parents' marriage—as far as I know, there had been no other children. Except for one school friend—and my classmates with whom I was, by and large, not very close—I grew up without other children my age. This probably explains why I've always been perfectly comfortable in my own company.

My parents came from very different backgrounds—one might almost say, cultures—and my aunt made her own rules. I came along after the Depression, too late to understand or identify with the world they had always known, and grew up in an England that bore little resemblance to the England they had lived in before WWI. Looking back at the generational, geographic, and personal distances between us, it's no wonder we all lived in separate worlds.

My father never talked about his early life and I could not identify with what my mother told me about hers. It was also standard practice in our house not to talk about family or, for that matter, any serious issues in front of "the child." I'm sure my parents meant well, but their secretiveness prevented me—deliberately or otherwise—from knowing much about my family, and from discovering the true cause or causes for the animosities and resentments all three had harbored towards each other for as long as I can remember.

My Parents

My maternal grandparents were second or third generation born and bred Berliners, with aristocratic pretensions and a value system to match. At least, that's how it always seemed to me—judging from the stories I heard and the mind-set they had passed on to their daughters. But perhaps that was the accepted norm in their day.

My grandfather owned a business making and selling linens. Along with their two daughters—my mother, Alice, and her younger sister Leah—they were decidedly more German than Jewish. They sent their daughters to the proper "Finishing Schools" for young ladies, spent their summers in fashionable spas or resorts, and their winters entertaining and attending concerts, plays, and "balls" with what I was told were the elite of Berlin Society. My mother never forgot those times, not even after the Depression had turned them into an average middle class family, and Hitler had driven us out of Berlin.

I know less about my father's family because my aunt, the major source of my information, had—with a few notable exceptions—preserved only her own family's letters and pictures. In recent years, my cousin—my father's niece and my sole remaining relative—was able to add a few factual bits and pieces and give me some interesting insights into my father's life. But she was born in London and had had only sporadic contact with him. Everything she knows had come from her mother, my aunt Mally, who had left Berlin in the early twenties, but had never lost touch with her brother.

As far as I have been able to find out, my father's family came from the Danzig (Gdansk) region. My grandfather's name—Siegfried Schidkowski—suggests both a Teutonic and a Polish connection. I have no other information about him. How he earned his living, what brought him to Berlin, how, when, and where he met my grandmother, Francesca Becker, is as much a mystery to me as the Becker family itself.

My father, Paul Albert, was born in 1873, the oldest (?) of Siegfried and Francesca's five girls and two boys. I've heard rumors that my grandparents were observant—perhaps even orthodox—Jews, but my father had become a free thinker early in life. For him, decency and integrity were always more important than money or religious and political affiliations. This was an admirable but unrealistic standard to which he clung all his life and which he resolutely applied to himself and everyone he met.

Studious, philosophical, and chronically out of touch with the practical world, my father would have thrived in a sheltered academic environment. But this does not seem to have been an option for him. With five sisters—his only brother had left home before him, and I don't know when my grandfather died—my father probably had had no choice but to go into business. Maybe that's why he chose to do so in Guatemala rather than a more competitive place like Berlin, London, or New York.

My parents met in some fashionable seaside resort in the summer of 1910. Since my father was by then an established businessman with a home in Guatemala, I assume he had come to Germany on business or to visit his family. I have not yet discovered what his business was or what had brought him to the seaside that day.

My mother's letters show that she was swept off her feet by the elegant, well traveled, sophisticated—and apparently wealthy—suitor fifteen years her senior. He was obviously smitten by her beauty. They were married in Berlin on July 1, 1911, three weeks before her twenty-second birthday. After a brief honeymoon in Italy, my father took her back to Guatemala.

My aunt saved all the letters my mother sent to her and my grandparents. Starting literally on her wedding day, my mother wrote home every single day, reporting in great— and sometimes embarrassing—detail what she had seen and done that day. Her letters describe, among many other things, her impressions of New York and New Orleans, her first encounter with a grapefruit aboard the ship to Belize, and enough about life in Guatemala to show that she was not happy there. Reading between the lines of her letters, one can readily see that her refined urban upbringing had simply not prepared her for the provincial—perhaps even rural—life in Guatemala. After the excitement of the wedding and the glamour of travel to new and distant places, Guatemala must indeed have been a huge disappointment for her—not to mention the language problem. My mother had also never been away from home before and openly missed her family. She seems to have tried to adjust, but in the end,—isolated, and inexperienced—she just couldn't do it.

Two years later, despite my father's candid reluctance to give up his home and livelihood, they moved to London, where he went into partnership with an English cousin. When

WWI broke out, my father sold his share of the business for the good of the company. Shortly thereafter, he was interned as an alien and spent he rest of the war in Knockalo, an internment camp on the Isle of Man. My mother went back to Berlin. After the war, my father was returned to Berlin where, following the Depression and subsequent Inflation, I was eventually born.

My Aunt Leah

The third member of my family, my aunt Leah, was unique—an Auntie Mame in combat boots. She never married, even though—judging from her photographs and the many admiring letters she had lovingly saved—she had been a strikingly beautiful young woman who had not lacked for suitors.

Having had to support herself all her life, Leah had acquired a number of marketable skills, a hard shell, tenacity, and a grim determination to let nothing—and no one—stand in her way. She knew what she wanted and how to get it, and never cared about stepping on people's toes or bending the truth. The truth, for Leah, was whatever would accomplish her purpose.

For as long as I can remember—and evidently dating back to years before I was born—there had been enmity between Leah and my father. I never got a credible explanation for it, and after all this time, I no longer care. But being single-mindedly devoted to my mother and me, Leah did as much for my father as she did for us. I did not know until long after they were all dead that she had looked after us when the Nazis made my father sell his business (whatever it was), and that she had continued to help us in London, when he found it hard to make yet another start in life.

Leah never cared about her personal appearance or conventional niceties. Much of the time, she looked like a bag lady, even though she had plenty of money and a closets full of respectable and even fashionable clothes. Her eccentric manners and careless appearance were a constant embarrassment for my socially conscious mother, and her morally questionable behavior infuriated my father, but Leah never changed.

Her stubbornness alone started endless fights in my house, but I think it must have been their indebtedness to her that made my parents resent her the most. They quarreled and fought with her whenever they got together, and all too often among themselves. My father never wavered in his hostility towards her, but my mother would side with or against her, depending on her mood or the issue in question. I know they each loved me in their own way, but they also wanted me to take sides, and I resented being put in the middle and persistently fought over. Eventually, I learned to handle the situation, but it took me years to realize that constant fighting was not an indispensable part of family life.

Despite the ongoing battles and personal abuse, my aunt never left us. Her selfless efforts on our behalf (and on behalf of other family members whom I never knew) were truly heroic and perhaps even foolhardy. But where her family was concerned, Leah's dedication was unwavering, and her devotion to us fierce and unshakable. Her exploits would merit an entire chapter on their own, and perhaps some day I'll write it.

Cousins and Others

It seems to me that my parents couldn't have had many friends, because we seldom had visitors or visited others. The few relatives I occasionally met in Berlin were always on my mother's side of the family and much older than I. At these meetings, I was invariably the only child present, ignored or fawned over by people I can neither remember nor identify now.

We had virtually no contact with my father's family. For reasons that were never convincingly explained to me, my mother didn't want to have anything to do with them. This was a pity because I had four cousins whom I hardly knew.

My father's sister, Else, had three sons, the youngest of whom was only a few years older than I. Another sister, Amalie (or Mally), had a daughter, Eleanor, some eight years my senior. I met the boys only once in Berlin, when we were all very little. When the persecutions began, my aunt and uncle escaped to France with the boys and went into hiding until the war was over. After my uncle passed away and the middle brother, Günter, died in a Russian labor camp (we may never know how or when), my aunt and her two surviving sons moved to South America. They are all gone now, of course—but at least I was able to meet Else and my youngest cousin, Heinz, once or twice before they passed away. Eleanor tells me that Ernst, the oldest, once visited London, but I don't remember meeting him.

Except for one accidental encounter in wartime London, I never met Eleanor until about 20 years ago, when she came to New York on business. Now we see each other at least once a year. An only child like me, Eleanor still talks about the three boys, who were like brothers to her in childhood, and close friends as adults. They kept in touch and visited each other for the rest of their lives. I missed all that.

Early Childhood

All I can remember of my early childhood are bits and pieces of three or four different flats in which we lived, but I only remember the addresses of two—one from when I was very small, and the other of the flat from which we left for London. Both buildings are still standing and occupied.

When I was in Berlin a few years ago, I instantly recognized the street—Darmstätter Strasse—and the house—Nr. 3— where we had lived when I was just tall enough to see over my mother's bed. I am convinced that if I had been able to enter the building, I could have found my way to "our" front door. I'm also convinced I still know the layout of the rooms and even where some of the furniture had stood. I would have loved to ring the bell and test my memory, but I was with a friend and we didn't have time to stop.

The nearby Preussenpark, which had seemed so huge when I was little, turned out to be a grassy area the size of a large city block. I instantly recognized the path around its perimeter from the photos I have of me walking there with our German shepherd, Rolf, and my mother behind us, taking pictures. The dog's back was about shoulder-high to me, and I'm wearing white shoes, white socks, a white hat, white gloves, and nothing else. My mother later told me that in those days people frequently let their small children go around undressed. I thought it prudent not to include photographic proof of that here.

Holidays

We were not observant Jews. In Berlin, my mother—like her parents before her—went to Synagogue three days a year, on the High Holidays. In London, she went a little more often. My father and I went only under duress.

The first school I ever went to—the one outside of which my Schultüten picture was taken—provided Hebrew lessons for its Jewish pupils. This is where I learned the Hebrew alphabet. The instructors must have been very good, because I can still read some of the letters, without of course understanding the words they form. In Golders Green, I went for a while to the Hebrew School at our local temple, but all I remember about it now is a smattering of Bible stories.

In my family, any kind of religious observance was, to say the least, casual. We knew we were Jewish—it was a simple fact and nothing more. My father, as I said earlier, was a philosopher who doubted the relevance of any dogma or "ism." My mother, I think, considered her occasional attendance at services more a social obligation than a religious duty. None of us spoke Hebrew—what few prayers and songs my mother and I sang during the services, we had learned by rote, without understanding the words.

We ate Matzos at Passover and lit Chanukah candles. I don't remember the Seders we must have held, but I always liked the sight and smell of the Menorah candles, and singing "Mowows Tsur"—as always, with no understanding of the words.

Given our secular lifestyle, it is not surprising that we also celebrated secular versions of Christmas and Easter. For us, these were children's holidays, devoid of religious significance. I don't remember getting Chanukah presents—maybe I did— but I clearly remember finding my presents under the tree.

We always had a Christmas tree in Berlin. It was decorated with colored glass ornaments, tinsel, live candles, and a star on top. One night one of the candles tipped over and ignited a branch. My father promptly put the fire out, but not before my terrified aunt had screamed, "Fire! Fire!" so loud and hysterically that the incident became one of my most vivid childhood memories.

Another Christmas Eve, when I was just tall enough to see across the dining-room table, Santa Claus came to dinner, wearing his red suit. He had a big round belly and a long white beard and I was delighted to meet him—until he shook my hand and I saw that he was wearing my father's ring. I never believed in Santa again.

To this day, the smell of pine reminds me of Christmas and the disappointments I still associate with it. Every year, I made out my wish list—writing to Santa was not a German custom and certainly not something I would have done after my "encounter" with him—and every year, very little came of it. My mother had definite ideas about toys, one of which was that girls play with dolls, and not with toy airplanes or trains.

Year after year, no matter how often I wished for a plane or a set of trains, I found dolls and beautiful dolls' dresses under the tree—even one year, a doll's bed with hand-embroidered sheets and pillowcases. I don't know what became of the bed after Golders Green, where the cat took it over to house her kittens, but I still have the doll with its hand-sewn dress. Like me, it has now acquired antique status.

I had to wait many years before I got to play with the toys I had always wanted. If my parents ever wondered why their teen-age daughter was lying on the living-room floor, happily playing with planes and toy soldiers with the eight-year-old son of a neighbor, they never mentioned it. In due course, living through the Blitz and the Battle of Britain updated and expanded my childhood feelings. After my son was born, I made a model of my favourite bomber, the B17. It was a labor of love, and I still get pleasure looking at it, even if a few bits and pieces have to be glued back on from time to time. I've never stopped collecting RAF books and pictures of the Battle of Britain, and I make a point of seeing movies and air shows that feature RAF and WWII planes. Some childhood fancies are slow to die.

At Easter time, my mother and I dyed dozens of hard boiled eggs, but I can't remember why or what we did with them. One Easter morning, my parents and I went for a walk in the nearby Grunewald, hunting for chocolate eggs. My father would walk a few steps ahead of me, looking for eggs in the underbrush, and calling out every few minutes, "Look! There's another one!" Then I'd rush over, pick it up, and put it in my basket. I didn't catch on for years how the eggs had got there. After we left Germany, we had no more Christmas trees, and I had outgrown Easter egg hunts.

The only truly secular holiday we observed was New Year's Eve, popularly called "Sylvester." The traditional food for the occasion was jelly doughnuts. When I was around three or four years old, a photographer took a picture of me wearing a paper hat, and smiling into the camera with my chin carefully placed on a tray of doughnuts. I can still feel him position my chin and feel the sugar on my skin. The picture subsequently graced the cover of some glossy magazine's New Year's Eve issue.

When I was small, my mother would wake me, but later I was allowed to stay up until midnight on New Year's Eve. When it was almost time, she brought out the doughnuts and then we did something called "Blei-giessen" which literally translated means "lead-pouring." ("Blei" = "lead," and "giessen" = "to pour.") The lead came in assorted small animal shapes. We usually had an assortment of them, always including several pigs because my mother said pigs were lucky. Each of us would then choose our piece, melt it on special spoons over a fire, and as soon as the lead had liquefied, pour it into a bowl of cold water. This instantly turned the sizzling lead into contorted shapes, which we would then "read" and interpret as omens for the future. We repeated the process until all the pieces were gone.

I have no idea how or where this practice began, but it seems to have been a widely practiced Sylvester tradition. Not long ago, rummaging through the attic, I came across a little "blei" pig that somehow escaped its fate. Now it lies on my souvenir shelf, awaiting an explanatory note for the next generation.

School

When I think of the millions of people who suffered and lost so much at the hands of the Nazis, I feel almost ashamed to admit that the only suffering I endured—and I truly remember it as such—was at the hands of my classmates.

I had always been fat and clumsy, and had learned very early in life that my mother's idea of "healthy-looking" meant "fat" to everyone else. Like other fat children, I was the butt of jokes, and always standing on the sidelines hoping for someone to come and play with me. They seldom did. One day on the playground, some children were playing "Zoo" asked me to be the fat pig. My mother promptly ran over and pulled me away, but I would have been happy to oblige.

In school, I couldn't keep up in gym classes or schoolyard games and everyone made fun of me. Later, it would be the same in London; only there they would make fun of my broken English as well.

By 1938, we had been living for some time in a flat on the Hohenzollerndamm, in the mixed, middle-class Grunewald section of Berlin. I remember it as almost a boulevard—tree lined, with streetcar tracks down the middle and stately apartment houses on both sides of the street. In bad weather, I took the streetcar to school, but on most days I walked or cycled there.

I had been enrolled in the Leonore Goldschmidt Schule on the Roseneck, a fairly prosperous residential neighborhood not far from our flat. The school was privately run and secularly Jewish— the only quasi-religious observance I can recall there was a Purim celebration for which my mother forced me to recite a poem I had written about Esther and Haman. It was torture!

Most of our classes were held in a converted mansion. The school's offices, auditorium and gym, were located in a big main building set back from the road by a large, sweeping lawn, on which we played and exercised. Here one day, when I was attempting the broad jump, my teacher declared to all and sundry that I ran "as if I had drunk buttermilk." I still don't know what the expression meant, but I knew it was no compliment.

Today, a large apartment block has replaced the main building and the sloping lawn. The only reminder of the school is a small plaque on the wall of a modest restaurant on the Hohenzollerndamm, built on what would have been the edge of the school's property.

I still remember the names of some of my schoolmates— Margit Zippert, Margit Rosenthal, and Steffi Lazarus, as well as Miriam Dobrin, whom I may however have met somewhere else—but my only close friend in school was my classmate Ellie Saalfeld. Ellie must have lived near us because we often spent our afternoons together. There was a small park near our apartment house, where we went skating in winter on flooded tennis courts. I was never very good at it—especially bundled up, as I was, in bulky clothes—but I managed to make a figure 8, which for me was quite an achievement. The park is still there, but the tennis courts are gone.

One of the things Ellie and I had in common was our love of sour pickles. Every day we'd pool some of our lunch-money and wander down to what would now be called a Deli near the Roseneck (there is still a small cluster of shops there) and bought ourselves a long sour pickle. The man behind the counter would split it lengthwise for us and wrap each half separately so we could eat it on the way back to school. I can still taste it—cold, crisp, and juicy. I suspect that's where I got my lifelong love of pickles.

I have only one small picture of Ellie—tall and gangly with bangs on her forehead. I don't know what became of her, and tried in vain to trace her.

I wish I could have said good-bye to her.

Time To Leave

Around 1935-6, even I became aware that Berlin was changing. There were Hitler rallies, political speeches, parades and strangely alarming newspaper reports. I especially remember the huge, spectacular display of Nazi pomp and pageantry at the opening ceremonies of the Olympic games, to which my parents had taken me. I think Hitler himself was there that night. The seemingly endless parade of Brown shirts, SS men, and Hitler Youths, the long red swastika banners, the torches, the martial music and the rousing speeches were both impressive and ominous. I didn't understand about Jesse Owens until much later.

My mother also took me to other Olympic events, including swimming and fencing, which I particularly enjoyed, and still remember vividly. The Games sparked my lasting interest in the ancient festival and would eventually take me to Olympia itself.

In due course, Germans were no longer allowed to associate with Jews. My mother had a life-long Christian friend, whose teenage children were now being questioned in school about their parents' social contacts. If it were to become known that their mother associated with Jews, their father, a career civil servant, would lose his job. The day came when my mother's friend asked us not to contact her anymore.

Around this same time, park benches began to be marked "For Jews only," and it was announced that Jews would henceforth have to wear yellow armbands. We must have left before that rule was enforced, because we never wore armbands. I remember wondering at the time how the Nazis could tell that we were Jewish: we looked just like everyone else.

These must have been anxious days for my mother, even though my father told us repeatedly that we had no reason for concern. Hitler, he said, was not after us because we were assimilated, non-practicing Jews. My mother, of course, knew better and it was thanks to her persistence that the three of us survived.

When the Nazis began confiscating Jewish passports, my mother ordered my father to London. Naturally, he objected and insisted that she was as always exaggerating the situation. But my mother broached no argument, and so my father left the following afternoon.

A few days later, an official envelope arrived for him. My mother held it up to the light and read "Pass-Angelegen-heiten"—passport matters. She forwarded the letter to my father in a plain white envelope, and he promptly wrote back, "Deiner war auch dabei." ("They wanted yours, too.") That night, we left Berlin.

The Journey

I can only imagine how my mother must have spent the first part of that day. By the time I came home from school, she had packed a small suitcase for me and was packing her own. She told me not to go out or call Ellie—we were going to go on a train-ride, she said, and it had to be a secret. Since my mother had taught me never to divulge anything that might incite someone's envy—"Envy invokes the Evil Eye," she always said—I assumed that she was planning some very special surprise for us.

During the afternoon I saw my mother take her grandmother's silver sugar bowl—a family heirloom and still one of my treasured possessions—and fill it with needles and spools of thread. It was the only thing of value she packed with a few clothes and enough food to see us to our destination. We left everything else.

I remember how excited I was to be going on a nighttime adventure. When the time came, we closed the door behind us, and took the streetcar to the central train station, the Bahnhof Zoo. I can still see the brightly lit billboard across the street from the platform, flashing "ZOO" in very large letters.

Once, when I was much younger, I had looked at that same sign and proudly announced to all and sundry that "Two Hundred means Zoo!" My mother must have thought that a brilliant remark because I heard her repeat it so often. But it was really an easy mistake for a child to make. I recently looked again at that same, still flashing sign, and with just a little imagination, the "Z" could indeed be interpreted—even by a grown-up—as a stylized "2."

I must have fallen asleep on the train because I can't remember anything about the trip, and it was daylight when we stopped at the border—I think it was at Aachen (Aix-la-Chapelle).

While we were waiting for the border guard to check our papers, my mother warned me not to say a word. In due course, a uniformed official came into the compartment. He asked to see my mother's passport (on which I was included), and told her to open our suitcases for inspection. "What's this?" he asked when he saw the sugar bowl. "Oh, that," my mother answered nonchalantly, "that's my sewing box."

The man must have suspected something—looking back on it now, I'm sure he did—but he just handed her the passport and left without another word. My mother pocketed the passport, and closed the suitcase with a sigh of relief. A short time later, the train lurched forward and we were free.

At Calais, we boarded the ferry to Dover. By then, it was night again, and we sat on the rolling deck, covered with blankets. The stars were bright and the rough Channel didn't bother us. We sat there enjoying our bread and salami to rather curious looks from the few distressed-looking people who had ventured up on deck. It might have been then that I first conceived the theory—long since disproved—that children don't get seasick.

In due course, we arrived in Dover.

Part Two: Memories of London

The Boarding House

I don't remember the landing or the train ride to London, but it was around 10:30 p.m. when we arrived at Victoria Station. My mother (who, I've just realized, must have had the foresight to bring some English money) promptly called my father.

"Where are you?" I heard him ask, listening in.

"At Victoria," replied my mother. My father was audibly delighted that we had made it safely out of Germany.

There was a vacancy in his boarding house, so we took a taxi to the place. On the way, I got my first glimpse of London, which even at that late hour was crowded and lit up with thousands of bright lights. I remember how excited I felt knowing I'd be living in such a magical place.

The boarding house was located in a residential neighborhood near a small park—according to my cousin, in the Notting Hill

Gate area. Wherever it was, we now found ourselves in what was to my 11-year old eyes a new and alien environment—a strictly kosher establishment. I have no idea how my unobservant father had come to live there.

All I remember about the place is the food. At breakfast, we were served corn flakes with warm milk, which was probably not a rule of Kashrus, but which I'm happy to say I've never encountered since. It was soggy and awful—I ate it only because I had been brought up to eat whatever was on my plate.

I don't recall lunches—maybe they didn't serve any—but the dinner entrees were planned according to the day of the week, and Thursday nights were Sausage nights.

Being German, we had our definite ideas about sausages. Some of my best childhood memories are of being treated to sausages and potato salad at the KaDeWe, which even then was the Harrod's of Berlin. My first bite into a sausage after my initial return to Berlin some years ago was Nirvana, and sausages of various kinds had been—and would continue to be—a staple in our house for as long as I could remember. So even at the tender age of eleven, I was familiar with hot dogs, salami, bratwurst and any other kinds of sausage known to Berliners. But neither my parents nor I had ever seen a strawberry-pink sausage.

It was not just their color—these sausages were tasteless, limp, soft-skinned, and just plain awful. The first Thursday, my parents tried to set a good example by eating them. They failed. The following week my mother, who had been brought up—like me—never to waste food, wrapped the sausages in a napkin and said she'll give them to some dog in the park.

My father strongly advised against it. "The next time that dog sees you," he said, "he'll bite you." It was one of the very few times I ever saw my mother throw food away, but perhaps pink sausages didn't really qualify as "food." They were certainly not worthy of being called sausages.

We must have moved out soon afterwards because I would have remembered other Thursday dinners. I never saw these pink sausages again in any butcher shop, kosher or otherwise, but then I never went looking for them.

Leah To The Rescue

Despite the steadily worsening situation in Europe, my aunt had continued to travel back and forth between London and Berlin on a regular basis. She happened to be in London when we arrived, and when she heard that we had just walked away from our flat, she promptly returned to Berlin. For her, property was sacrosanct and leaving property to the Nazis was unthinkable.

Rules and regulations had never applied to Leah—as far as I can see, she had either ignored or circumvented them all her life. In the pre-war years, when nobody was allowed into the UK without a sponsor or a waiting job, she carried several sets of papers, variously describing her as a nurse, a secretary, a housekeeper and a business representative. The skills were real, and in some cases, the names may have been real, but as far as I know, the waiting jobs were largely, perhaps even entirely, fictitious. If some immigration official refused her entry, she simply turned around, stayed out of sight for a few minutes, and then presented an alternate set of papers to another inspector. She always got in.

Later in the war, she applied the same brazen courage to obtain the needed forms for getting a distant cousin out of Germany. But that's another story.

Back in Berlin, undaunted by storm troopers and increasing violence against Jews, Leah moved into our apartment and packed up not only everything belonging to my mother and me, but also her own belongings, including all the family papers and photographs dating back at least a hundred years. But she only took two tables and a chair that had belonged to my father's parents. I've always suspected she had included these three pieces not for my father's sake but because there had been room in the crate: Leah never wasted anything.

Having left detailed instructions with the movers, my aunt returned to London and successfully applied for permanent residence. A short time later, she had moved into a flat near us. That must have been late '38 or early '39.

The care and attention Leah had devoted to packing paid off: all but one crate—a victim of Allied bombs—arrived safely. Not a cup was chipped, and all the family papers were intact. They continue to be my biggest source of information about my mother's family. I subsequently discovered that Leah had also, with commendable foresight, identified many people in the boxes of family photographs she saved. Thanks to her, I think I'll be able to identify the rest.

Throughout her stay in Berlin, Leah regularly sent us packages of salami and other German delicacies, and always included a few Marzipan bars for me. Leah, who had a mouthful of incurably sweet teeth, had loved chocolate—and especially marzipan—since her childhood and couldn't believe that I didn't like it as much as she. It would take me years to persuade her not to ply me with marzipan, but I suspect she never quite understood how anyone could prefer sour pickles to marzipan.

Our House

After the boarding house, we lived in a series of furnished rooms, all located in or around Golders Green, a still-to-this-day largely Jewish suburb in northwest London. Early in 1939, my parents bought the semi-detached house on Hendon Way, in which I lived until February 1948, when I left for New York. In 1950, my parents sold the house and followed me. Not long thereafter, my aunt followed all of us.

The architecture and layout of our house were the same as those of all the other semi-detached houses on our street and on thousands of similar streets all over England, distinguished from their neighbors' only by the number on the door, the style and color of the curtains, and the flowers in their front yards.

Our plumbing and heating facilities would be judged sub-standard—maybe even primitive—today, but in the 1940s they were standard equipment for houses like ours. We had a gas stove and a coal-burning water heater in the kitchen, and rarely used fireplaces in the two downstairs rooms. But we used freestanding gas heaters instead, so we would have more coal for hot water. The coal we got was not always good or easy to come by during the war, and much to my father's annoyance, had to be ordered weeks, sometimes even months, in advance. The bedrooms were always unheated, and during severe winters it was not unusual for a sheet of ice to form on a bedside glass of water.

None of the pipes in our unheated attic were insulated. Every autumn, my father crawled up there and wrapped them in old sheets and blankets, but it seldom did much good: the pipes froze when the temperature dropped and burst when it went up again. Almost every spring, we had water leaks and mildew damage on the walls. And every spring, my parents made the necessary repairs and Life went on.

Our house had a walk-in pantry and no refrigeration. Some people—including my Aunt—lived in "luxury flats," so-called because they had refrigerators, but Leah never turned hers on because she was afraid of the noise the motor made.

We never owned an icebox, let alone a refrigerator. In summer, my mother kept the milk cool by submerging the bottle in water. Perishable foods were rarely a problem because when you go shopping every day—as everyone then did—there is seldom enough food on hand to spoil.

Ice cream might have presented a problem, but I never saw ice cream in bulk. The only ice cream I knew came in single servings rolled in paper. It had a pasty, Vanilla flavored taste and was often served with a reasonable facsimile of apple pie at Lyons Corner Houses, a popular restaurant chain in London. Not knowing anything better, I considered Lyons' apple pie and ice cream a rare treat.

In those pre-supermarket days, people—at least in Golders Green—went in one direction to the butcher's, in another to the bakers' and in yet another for dairy foods, fish, cat food (fish heads), and sundries. I did a lot of errands on my bike and the electric tram stopped at the corner in case we needed a ride. But most of the time we walked. We were lucky to be living at the bottom of a hill, because that made it lot easier to carry the bags home.

Our house had a small, fenced-in front yard, a garden in the back (also fenced) and—between the houses—a narrow passage leading to the back door. There was no room for a garage—these houses were built long before cars became widespread. We only knew one person who owned a car, and we thought him immensely rich. Today, when almost everyone in England drives and street parking is frequently impossible, many Londoners have sacrificed the flowers, removed their fences, and turned their front yards into parking spaces.

Just behind our garden was an open "Allotment" area in which people grew fruits and vegetables, which were hard to get during the war. I think the only vegetable we could readily obtain was cabbage. Someone once remarked that the English "only know three kinds of vegetables, and that two of them are cabbage." That was fine with me—I've always liked cabbage.

One day, a neighbor gave us one strawberry he had grown. We cut it up and carefully divided it between us.

Learning English

My mother had taught me a few words of English in Berlin, but having to speak it was an entirely different matter. My first few weeks and months in London were full of embarrassing moments. My contemporaries laughed at my bumbling efforts, and the harder I tried to communicate, the more flustered I got, and the more mistakes I made.

At that time, the "King's (or now the Queen's) English" was the standard, and the English, rightly proud of their language, tended to look down on foreigners who did not speak it well. When the war started, ridicule became hostility: they were English, I was German, and England was at war with Germany. There seemed to be nothing more to be said. But as the war went on and the bombs started falling on everyone, most people realized that we were all in the same boat, and the situation improved.

I don't remember how long it took me to learn English, but I must have mastered the basics fairly quickly, because a short time later, I was enrolled in the nearby Wessex Gardens Elementary School and as far as I can recall, able to handle the work.

School

After leaving Wessex Gardens, I went to the Secondary County Council School in Mill Hill, a short bus-ride away. I hated it from Day One. For one thing, the school was big on all forms of athletics, which I—still fat and clumsy—couldn't do. I dreaded the Gym periods and hid in an empty classroom until a teacher found me one day and reported me to our Dickensonian headmistress, Mrs. Schofield. From then on, Mrs. Schofield personally saw to it that I attended every gym class. I will never forget my embarrassment at not being able to lift myself up on—let alone vault over—the horse.

On the playing field, the game of choice was Rounders, which is essentially Baseball without the bells and whistles. I managed to hit the ball, but the less said about my running around the bases, the better.

My second clash with the school was over the school uniforms, which, despite the traditional unpredictability of the English climate, were changed by the calendar, not by the weather.

I hated the navy and green winter outfits, the heavy, dark blue pinafore with its broad box pleats, tied with a green sash belt. I looked and felt like a blimp. The pinafore was worn with navy woolen bloomers that kept bunching up the skirt, a long-sleeved white shirt with a green tie and a round felt hat with a green band. The summer uniforms were shapeless but less odious shifts of yellow or light blue gingham checks, with matching bloomers, and a gray straw hat.

Every morning, we had to file past Mrs. Schofield for inspection. One very warm spring day that was still officially "winter," I didn't wear my bloomers. Mrs. Schofield caught me—she probably noticed how much thinner I suddenly looked—and kept me after school. Again.

When the air raids began, the school was ordered to evacuate everyone to the country. This was my chance to get away. I stood my ground and spent the rest of the war in London.

But of course, I had to go to school. First, I was sent—I have no idea how or why—to the Settrington School, a private upper class school located (I think) somewhere in Hampstead. All I can now remember of it is being cast as a lady-in-waiting in some school play. I had no lines to speak—I just had to stand at the back of the stage and smile. The picture of me standing there in a long purple gown, looking fat, awkward, and out of place is a pale reflection of how I felt.

After the Settrington School, my mother enrolled me in the Willesden Polytechnic Institute, a high school for art and design that taught dressmaking and crafts, along with some Fine Arts and a smattering of academic subjects.

Sending me to Art School had not been my idea—I never had (and still don't have) much aptitude for Art or Design. But my mother, who had at one time wanted me to become a doctor, told me that she knew someone whose daughter was a "designer-cutter" and that "anything her daughter can do, you can do."

This was not the best way to choose anyone's career, but it worked out well enough for me, primarily because this was where I met Ellen Rozanski, who had, and still has, far more talent than I will ever have. Despite the disparity in our respective abilities, Ellen and I became friends.

Among the classes we shared was Life Drawing, a subject in which I actually did quite well because it didn't require any creativity to copy what was in front of me.

The problem with Life Drawing in wartime was that young models were hard—and as the war went on, virtually impossible—to find. The young men were in uniform, and the women either in factories or also in the armed forces. Our models were usually past middle age, and not exactly inspiring to draw.

But one morning, I walked into the classroom and saw a sleek young back, topped by a long, red, and beautifully styled, pageboy haircut.

"Great!" I said to Ellen, who had already set up her easel, "A young woman at last."

Ellen turned to me and quietly said, "I don't think so."

And sure enough, when the figure turned around, it was definitely not that of a woman, and underneath the expertly applied make-up he needed a shave.

That was how we met Quentin Crisp, an unabashed transvestite, then earning extra cash as a model. After the war, he became a well-known raconteur and writer, whose autobiography, *The Naked Civil Servant,* was later made into a movie starring John Hurt. But during the war he was just a thoroughly nice person who frequently modeled for us, and became everyone's friend.

After the War, Quentin moved to New York, where he starred in his own one-man show, talking about his life and experiences. I met him again when he took his show to Boston, but Ellen, who lived in New York, remained in touch with him until his death in 1999.

We also received a smattering of musical training at Willesden. It was administered by our blonde music teacher, Mrs. Denman, who decided one day to form a choir for which all of us had to audition. I—who still can't hold a note—turned out to be one of the only three altos in the class. Mrs. Denman placed me between the other two in the hope—or expectation—that their voices would somehow coax the right notes out of me. I'm never quite sure that they did—I could never tell sharp from flat—but Mrs. Denman, desperate for altos, kept me in the choir.

On some long-forgotten occasion, there was a performance of Smetana's "Moldau." I can't remember what this orchestral piece had to do with our choir, but to this day, I know every note of the "Moldau," and whenever I hear it, I think of Mrs. Denman and see myself on the riser, watching her direct us.

I don't remember graduating from Willesden and have not found any diploma from there, but I think Ellen and I must have completed the program. I know it was before the War ended. We remained friends, and visited each other regularly, often with our parents. One year, when we were about 19, Ellen and I went on holiday to Dover and Hastings. Around that time, I somehow—miraculously—slimmed down to a size 12.

Ellen emigrated to America only a few months after I did. Eventually, we both got married and lost touch. Quite some time thereafter, Ellen tracked me down and our friendship resumed.

Wartime

Britain declared war on Germany on September 3, 1939, a very hot Sunday morning. We were at home that day, the radio was on, and I was ironing by the open door to the garden. My mother was semi-dressed in the kitchen, and my father was reading the paper.

Mr. Chamberlain had no sooner announced that we were now at war with Germany than the sirens sounded. The authorities were probably just testing their equipment, but we had no idea what to expect or what we were supposed to do. My father, unruffled as always, returned to his paper, but my mother panicked and rushed upstairs, babbling something about her jewelry. A few minutes later, she came down again, with her gas mask and several necklaces around her neck, carrying a pillowcase with whatever valuables she had been able to grab. She was still in her underwear.

The All Clear sounded a few minutes later. My mother quickly recovered her composure and before long, we had all learned to take sirens in stride.

In anticipation of gas attacks, the authorities fitted everybody with gas masks in brown cardboard boxes that we had to carry with us at all times. The inside of the mask smelled of rubber, and was insufferably hot. Occasionally, there'd be impromptu drills, when we dutifully donned our masks, and waited to take them off again. Fortunately, we never needed them.

Blackout and safety regulations were rigorously observed and enforced. We taped every windowpane with masking tape to prevent flying glass and replaced our curtains with drapes made from special blackout material that kept out every chink of light. We hung blankets and carpets across the windows for extra protection, and turned out all the lights before opening the front door. Outside, we carried specially masked flashlights to find our way along pitch-dark streets, wore white or light clothing, and carried newspapers to make us more visible to each other.

Air-raid wardens, patrolling the streets, made sure that everyone observed the rules and when necessary, rescued people from bombed buildings. When people living in two-story houses were told to sleep downstairs. I moved into the Front Parlor for the rest of the war. My parents slept in the back room.

Although the suburbs were never hit as badly as the City, our neighbourhood was repeatedly bombed during the Blitz. We lived close to one of the big De Havilland Aircraft factories, which the Nazis tried night after night to destroy. But the factory was so well camouflaged that the Nazis never hit it and bombed the surrounding streets instead. Our house was one of those that were severely damaged several times but never completely destroyed. Our roof was repeatedly damaged, windows blown out and ceiling plaster—and more than once the ceilings themselves—rained down on us on a regular basis. But the structure itself held up.

After each raid, the authorities sent people to board up the windows and help make stop-gap repairs, so we could go on living in the house. There would be no permanent repairs as long as the raids continued.

One night during the Blitz, after I had gone to sleep, the house across the street got a direct hit. I heard the crash, but having heard crashes on a nightly basis, simply turned over and went back to sleep. My parents rushed into the room, found the blankets and carpet torn to shreds, and me in bed, covered with ceiling plaster. They thought I was dead. Great rejoicing when I sat up and wondered what all the fuss was about! We promptly celebrated my "survival" by opening a precious tin of pineapple given to us by an American soldier.

Another time, the Germans sent us series of incendiary bombs. Night after night, we saw burning houses on the other side of the allotments, and in the distance, the sky was orange from fires raging in the City.

On one such night, the incendiaries started falling while my father was in the bath. I should explain that the coal burner in the kitchen (after repeated stoking and assorted acts of encouragement) took about three or four hours to make a tub-full of hot water. When it finally reached the desired temperature, postponement for any reason was not an option.

So there was my father, sitting in the tub, while fires were lighting up the neighborhood. My mother frantically banged on the bathroom door, begging him to get out of the water. "If a bomb falls into the tub," replied my unflappable father, "it will go out." A tub of hot water was not something one wasted.

In due course, every house was provided with a shelter. There were two kinds, Anderson and Morrison—I forget which was which. I don't know how ours was delivered or installed, but it was certainly not set up by my father.

In the recent PBS series "The 1940's House," the man of the house had to dig his own foundation, assemble the pieces, and install the shelter himself. That was certainly not the case with us. Our shelters, like those of everyone we knew, were delivered and installed for us, first in the garden, and later, indoors.

The outdoor shelters were used only for a short time because they leaked and required frequent pumping out. Everything left in them—food, blankets, books, etc.—became damp and, in no time at all, moldy. We ended up emptying our shelter every morning, and moving everything back into it at night.

Soon, these useless shelters were replaced by large and formidable steel boxes—ours took nearly half of the front room—and remained in place until the end of the war. It had three sides of solid steel and a mesh "flap" that was fastened from the inside. These shelters, we were told, would hold up even if the whole house collapsed on top of it. Fortunately, ours was never put to the test.

On the other hand, comfort was not one of its strong points. There was plenty of room to stretch out but not to sit up. The floors were hard and, being steel, cold. But at least we were dry, and whatever my mother put in there—rugs, blankets, and valuables—could be left in place. I can still feel my father's bony elbow digging into me while both of us giggled nervously at the noisy air raid going on outside. My mother, lying on my other side, found nothing amusing about it.

Then there was the rationing. Almost everything was rationed sooner or later during the war. We didn't own a car, so the gasoline and tire rationing didn't affect us—our concerns were with food and clothing.

Everybody was issued a ration book, which had to be presented whenever we bought rationed foods, so that the shopkeeper could cut out the relevant coupons. As best I recall, we were allowed 2 oz. of butter and cheese a week, two or three eggs, and a certain amount of meat, bacon, milk and sweets.

The introduction of sweets rationing launched Leah on monthly bartering trips that took her to various parts of London, whenever our sweets were running low. She knew exactly who would barter what and where, and always returned with a couple of chocolate bars. We accepted and ate them gratefully, and asked no questions.

Clothes rationing worked on a points system. Everybody was allotted a certain number of points per month. Every item of clothing cost points—more for a coat, say, than for a pair of socks, and so on. Once you had spent all the points, you couldn't buy anything else until next month. We learned to "Make Do and Mend" and be as inventive as possible with what we could get.

Social Life and Beyond

During the war, we were referred to as "Aliens" or "Enemy Aliens." Unable to blend in, we found companionship and support in our own social or religious clubs and youth groups.

My parents belonged to a neighborhood Club organized and run by German refugees. My mother attended social functions there and my father had his partners for his beloved Chess and Bridge. I joined a club for young Germans who met regularly in a large house somewhere near Willesden. I don't know who owned the house, but several of our members, including one married couple, lived on the upper floors, and presumably had some arrangement with the landlord to keep the building in good order. Our meetings were strictly social—dropping in for a chat or a cup of tea, listening—and sometimes dancing—to records and singing songs. Now and then, some speaker would come and talk to us on various subjects, and there was the occasional party.

It was here, one New Year's Eve, that I first heard "Auld Lang Syne" and, linking arms to the music, was swept up by the camaraderie. I still enjoy hearing the song; perhaps because it reminds me that I met the first boy I ever dated at that party. His name was Martin, and he was tall and had black curly hair.

Ellen tells that we also joined a Jewish youth group, the Habonim, about which I remember absolutely nothing. But I do recall a raw, rainy weekend in a soggy tent on a stubble field somewhere near London. This, is seems, had been a Habonim-sponsored outing on which Ellen and I had gone together. All I remember about it, apart from the misery of the weather, was walking through stubble, my legs scratched and bleeding, trying to bunch up some cut grass or hay. I've not slept in a tent since.

Late in the war, Hitler launched his V-I ("Doodle Bug") rockets and then the V-2s. Ellen and I saw our first "Doodle Bug" one sunny morning from the entrance of our school shelter. I looked at its fiery tail and first thought it was a burning plane trying to get home. But "Doodle Bugs" were, in fact, unmanned missiles programmed to hit a specific target. Their engines, which made a very distinctive "putt-putt" sound, were timed to cut out when the missiles reached the calculated angle from which they then dived into their targets. You soon learned that if the engine stopped directly overhead, you were safe, but if it stopped before it got to you, you dived for cover and waited for the crash.

The V-2s, on the other hand, struck randomly and without warning. Since you couldn't protect yourself against them, you did your best to ignore them. Now and then, on the way to or from work, I'd see a V-2 hit a building and explode.

When VE-Day arrived, I was among the crowds celebrating the Allied victory on Piccadilly Circus. All traffic leading into the Circus was closed off, and people were crowded into every corner cheering, waving flags and hugging each other. The war in Europe was over, and our shared wartime experiences had given me a strong and lasting sense of belonging.

Over the years, London has changed enormously. Today, London is a polyglot city in which ever fewer people speak traditional English. A varied mix of foreign accents has taken its place and ethnic multiplicity is taken for granted. The city has also become a haven for the young—the vast majority of today's Londoners never knew wartime—let alone pre-War—London. But I feel a happiness there that I don't feel anywhere else.

Work

I know I started working while we were still being bombed because I often passed newly bombed houses on the way to the Nr.113 bus, which I took to two of my three jobs. I rode my bicycle to the third, located in Camden Town.

Having supposedly been trained as a "Designer-Cutter" and having no other marketable skills, I naturally gravitated towards work in the garment-trade. I can't remember how I found my jobs, but all the people I had worked for were good people who treated me well, and seemed not to notice what was so obvious to me—my lack of talent and enthusiasm. Either I was better than I thought, or just incredibly lucky.

I started my first job at Auerbach & Steinitz while taking watercolor classes at the Regent Polytechnic Institute on Regent Street. I wasn't very good with watercolors, but I liked the medium and again, had no problem copying what was in front of me. This made my foray into watercolors a limited success. I ultimately painted five or six still lifes, which still hang in my house, the source of much inner satisfaction. They are the only paintings I ever produced, and I love them not because they are good, but because they are mine.

Auerbach & Steinitz was also located on Regent Street, almost across the street from the "Regent Poly." Its small staff custom-made dresses that were individually assembled by hand. I was apprenticed to one of the dressmakers, a spindly lady called Stimmy, who also initiated me—being the newest and lowest level employee—into the tea-making ritual: warm the pot, steep the tea, and then, after putting the sugar and milk into the cup—strictly in that order— pour the tea and serve. Put cozy over teapot to keep it warm. After the tea break, wash the dishes and put them away.

When I wasn't making tea, I was handing Stimmy one pin after another while she draped, pinned, and basted the dress on the manikin. We had manikins in all the stock sizes, and for those customers who couldn't fit any of them there were wire ones, that were molded directly on the customer by someone high up in the ranks, whom I never saw. After the first fitting, Stimmy would make the adjustments and send the dress back for the second fitting. Eventually, the dress was assembled. Stimmy did all the sewing, including the buttonholes. Initially, I only did the finishing, cutting off all the loose threads and oversewing every seam by hand. Eventually, I was allowed to do some of the sewing myself. I didn't realize it at the time, but I was being taught the finest dressmaking techniques in the field. I soon started to make my own clothes in the same meticulous manner, and until a few years ago, when I stopped sewing, everything I wore had to be hand-finished.

My next job was for Max Gerstel, who owned "Molly Modes, Ltd.," a small wholesale dress factory in Camden Town. The very antithesis of Auerbach & Steinitz, Molly Modes mass-produced inexpensive dresses, many bearing the "Utility" label, a logo indicating that the garment met official wartime standards. This is where I learned to make, grade, and lay out patterns, and cut out dresses in bulk.

Mr. Gerstel was a rough-cut, straight-talking quintessential "Mensch," who cared about the people who worked for him. But what still endears him to me is the fact that that he gave me his and all his family's cheese rations. The Gerstels were orthodox and bought all their food from "strictly kosher" stores in the East End. But for some reason Mr. Gerstel didn't quite trust the purity of the cheese, so he gave it to me instead. Being a cheese lover subsisting on two ounces of cheese a week, I asked no questions and gratefully accepted his gesture.

My last job in London—now as a somewhat experienced, but still untalented and unenthusiastic pattern maker and cutter—was for a modest-sized dress firm on Clifford Street, off Bond Street. The house no longer exists, and I have no idea what became of the business and its owner, Mr. Goldberg. Max Goldberg was an ex-refugee, married to an Englishwoman and, like Mr. Gerstel, a pleasure to work for. But the quality of Mr. Goldberg's dresses far exceeded that of Molly Modes, Ltd and almost matched the haute couture of the Bond Street boutiques.

We had a small staff—a designer, a pattern maker and cutter (me), the office staff (Mrs. Goldberg and two secretaries), and a small number of salesmen. The dresses were assembled in factories off the premises—I had little to do with that part of the business.

I have fond memories of my Clifford Street days—we were almost a family. When Princess Elizabeth, as she was then, married Prince Philip in November 1947, we all stopped working and listened to the ceremony on the radio. On Christmas Eve, Mr. Goldberg threw us all a party, and now and then, invited us all to an impromptu get-together. He even hand-delivered my salary when I was too sick to come to work. (In those days, I was so asthmatic that I often couldn't get out of bed in the cold weather.)

One "bonus" of being a cutter was the possibility of finding a way to lay out a pattern so that a large piece of the yardage was left uncut. Since leftover pieces were routinely thrown out, I could keep the ones I wanted. For much of the war, I eked out my clothes rations by making dresses from these leftover pieces. To judge from the pictures of me wearing some of these creations, I was quite good at it.

If I had not left for New York in February 1948, I would probably have gone on working for Mr. Goldberg. It was easy, I enjoyed the atmosphere, and I felt comfortable doing the work. More importantly, I didn't know what else to do. I had always known that I did not belong in the dress business, and had simply taken the path of least resistance. But as I approached my twenty-first birthday, I knew I wanted to do something more with my life. I need to find answers and I knew by now that I'd never find those answers as long as I was living at home.

So—one thing led to another, and in due course, I arrived in New York.

Marcelle's
Photo
Album

Berlin
London
Cliftonville

Grollman Strasse 57, where my grandparents and their daughters lived. The house no longer exists. My mother and grandmother can be seen on the balcony. (c. 1905).

Formal Wedding Picture of my parents, Alice and Paul. July 1, 1911.

My aunt Leah. (c. 1915).

Me at fourteen months.

"Happy New Year." Picture of me on a magazine cover c. 1930.

My first day of school (Volksschule 14. Berlin Schmargensdorf. 1932?) The paper cone filled with sweets and called a Schultüte was a German first-day-of-school tradition.

My mother and I.

Two new schoolmates and I enjoying a treat from a popular dairy company truck.

The apartment block on the Hohenzollerndamm.
Nr. 64 was the middle door and our flat is on the
second floor left.

Classmate Margit Zippert, left and Ellie Saalfeld.
This is my only picture of Ellie (c. 1937).

Our house in Hendon Way,
with my parents.

My parents and I at our front door. (c. 1946).

Two pictures of my parents. (c. 1945).

Aunt Leah, my mother and I in the front parlour.
(c. 1947?).

Portion of my sketches of Quentin Crisp. c. 1947.
Autographed by him. c. 1991.

Me with my mother's friend, Frau Scholz,
Berlin. c. 1938.

Ellen and I in
Cliftonville. 1947.

Me at Coney Island, 1948.

Postscript

It's been over half a century since I sailed into New York harbor aboard the "Queen Mary," past the Statue of Liberty and up the West Side of Manhattan. In the weeks that followed, I found an acceptable job in the garment district, working for a large sportswear manufacturer. It paid my expenses. Before the year was up, I found what I had been looking for, changed jobs, and started working my way through school. In due course, I became an American citizen and finally, a person in my own right.

I now have a home and family here, but deep down, I feel I still don't quite belong, and probably never will. To some extent, this is the product of my own isolated and idiosyncratic upbringing, but I think it is also in large part the result of being uprooted in childhood, an experience I share with many former refugees.

The Fates may have been immeasurably kinder to us than to millions of others, but even though our survival has allowed us to adapt to—and successfully adopt—substitute identities, we have nonetheless lost a fundamental part of our selves, and nothing we or anyone else can do, will ever restore it.

In that respect, we are all Hitler's victims.

Daisy Rubin Roessler

Daisy Rubin Roessler

Daisy Rubin was born in Vienna, Austria, in 1926. In 1932 she moved with her family to Berlin.

When all Jewish children had to leave German Elementary schools, she was transferred to the Fasanenstrasse Religious school, where she and Ellen Rozanski first met at the age of seven. They have remained lifelong friends.

In 1937 they both enrolled in the Addas Yisroel Lyceum for Jewish girls, and in 1939 Daisy was put on a Kindertransport to England by her parents. That was the end of Daisy's formal education.

Her parents fortunately also escaped the Nazis, and arrived in London just as World War II was beginning. Daisy joined them in 1942, and worked in the garment trade, while studying pattern-making in night school. She married Mendel Roessler in 1949, and they opened a successful dress factory together.

In 1979 she and Mendel retired to Israel where she did volunteer work for various organizations.

After her husband's death she moved to Ra'anana, to be near her family She has one married daughter, Susan, three grandchildren and is the proud great-grandmother of four lively little girls.

DAISY RUBIN ROESSLER - CONTENTS

Episodes—Impressions—Moments

Daisy Rubin Roessler

1) I used to love going to KaDeWe in the Tauentzin Strasse. On the sixth floor they had a Kosher Department where my mother bought me wieners and mustard on a cardboard plate with a tiny wooden fork. It was a great treat. I used to collect the forks.

2) The Nazis forbade the Jewish method of slaughtering animals. My father had a cousin in Budapest who used to send us brown paper parcels containing raw chicken quarters through the post. I remember those greasy parcels as though it were yesterday.

3) My father did not sleep at home on 9th November 1938. The new office manager who had been put in charge (as only "Aryans" were allowed to be in managerial positions) was a member of the Nazi Party, complete with S.A. uniform, and he told my dad *not* to sleep at home that night.

4) We were a traditionally observant family and visited the Passauerstrasse synagogue on Saturdays. Many times the Hitler Youth boys and girls stood there and shouted:

Jude, Jude, Jude, Raus aus Eurer Bude.
[Jew, Jew, Jew, Get out of your hovel.]

5) Before my brother was born, and before the Anschluss in March 1938, we were foreign nationals, having Austrian passports. During the years before that date I remember different men sleeping over. They must have been people with Polish passports who were hunted by the Germans and sent over the border in the most terrible manner.

6) We lived in a large apartment block. The landlady also lived there. She told my parents she could no longer greet them on the stairs as her son had joined the SS. Neither was the concierge's little boy allowed to play with me any more.

7) Ellen and I were best friends from the age of six and we attended each other's birthday parties. At one of them I offered to help and pushed the trolley piled high with goodies along the corridor. It overturned and everything spilled on to the floor. Ellen and her sister Silvia had "Shirley Temple" curls. She was my favorite actress. I was absolutely devastated that, as a Jewess, I could no longer visit the cinema.

8) My mother had all her clothes, dresses, hats, gloves, etc. hand-made. The dressmaker for her "afternoon dresses" was a white Russian Countess. She had very thin hair draped over her skull. She wore lots of bracelets and brooches, as well as long gold chains around her neck. She was always wearing thick make-up and bright red lipstick. She lived and worked in one room. There were

always women in various stages of undress sitting around. She used to talk about the Soviets as if they were the devil incarnate and said she preferred the Germans. But then she was not Jewish. I loved going there. She used to let me play with bits of material, buttons, feathers, etc. She was also an exceptional dressmaker.

9) To sum up, as a Jewish child in pre-war Nazi Germany, I felt like I was standing in front of a closed door, with everyone inside enjoying themselves while I was unable to participate.

From Vienna and Berlin via England to Israel

I was born in Vienna, Austria in 1926 and moved with my parents to Berlin, Germany in 1932. My father's firm manufactured electric heating pads filled with sand to which radium elements were added. His company also made Samovar-like containers that were filled with water to which radium elements were added and allowed to stand overnight. This mixture was drunk the next morning. It was guaranteed to relieve rheumatic pains.

His firm decided to open a branch in Berlin where my father managed the entire enterprise. The firm received many letters from grateful customers.

In April 1932, I was due to start school. So, dressed to kill—my mother was a great follower of fashion—and holding a *Schultuete* (a multicolored conical cardboard container filled with goodies), I set off for school, along with my mother and Elfride our maid, for my first day at school.

The children lined up in the Great Hall and waited for the "Welcome to School" speech. While waiting in line, the girl standing next to me whispered, "My mother says you killed our Lord Jesus and I must never talk to you, or even stand next to you!" I had never heard of her Lord Jesus, let alone killed him, so I answered, "I have not learned about that yet." And that was my introduction to the school system in Berlin.

Our teacher was a youngish, blonde woman who had a very large brooch graced by a Swastika pinned to her very ample bosom. She never spoke normally to Jewish children. Instead, she shouted at us and made us look foolish. During Bible studies, Jewish children had to stand outside the classroom door and were not allowed to talk.

It was a big relief to me when Jewish children were sent to Jewish facilities and taught by Jewish teachers who had been forced to leave their jobs at German (Aryan) schools. We went to classrooms in the community center of the Fasanenstrasse Synagogue. We children were between the ages of 6 and 11. Hundreds of us started having lessons there. Our teachers were the cream of the crop who had PhD degrees and were university professors. They'd been reduced to teaching us ABCs and our "1, 2, 3s."

Daily, some teachers or children did not turn up for lessons. Even we little kids started to get an inkling of impending evil. We were asked to drop spare sandwiches, fruit, even cash into a special box in the school yard for children whose breadwinner fathers had been taken away. Most of them were never seen again.

At home there were also changes. Elfriede, the maid, and Frau Genscher, the washer-woman, had to leave our employ. They were not allowed to work for Jews. Frau Genscher, an ardent communist, took our washing home to Neukoelln. This act must have been her personal act of resistance to the Nazis.

We kept a Kosher home but soon it was forbidden to slaughter meat according to Jewish law. One kept a low profile when going to synagogue, cinemas, theaters, concerts, etc. because we were labeled *Judenschweine* (Jew Pigs). No sitting on park benches for Jews. I had a yearly membership card for the zoo, but that was no longer allowed for Jews. When going to school or traveling on the train, one frequently heard, *Judenkind, geh nach Palestina* (Jew child go back to Palestine) with a few stones thrown. Jewish boys got worse treatment. They were beaten up regularly.

Meanwhile my parents tried desperately to obtain a visa to anywhere else in the world that would enable our family to leave Germany. I can still see my father sitting at the dining room table under a lamp with a green shade writing letter after letter.

In July 1937, my mother gave birth to a baby boy, so it was decided to return to Austria as soon as possible. Because we had Austrian citizenship that was no problem. But the "Anschluss" in March 1938 changed all that. Overnight we were "Stateless".

My grandfather in Vienna was taken to the Dachau concentration camp. He was killed there and, to add insult to injury, his ashes were sent to his wife, my grandmother. She was informed that he had died of "natural causes" and she could have his remains for the payment of 10 Marks. Actually, he is the only family member buried in Vienna. All the other family members were taken to Auschwitz during the war and were never heard from again.

In 1937, I transferred to the Jewish Girls Lyceum in Siegmundshof, Berlin. It meant a 50-minute walk to and from school but I preferred that to being jostled on the train. The German children used to shout, *Juden raus, Ihr verpestet unser Deutschland!* (Jews out, you poison our Germany!)

After the Kristallnacht in November 1938, my parents heard from a friend about a scheme to send children to England on their own. They would be looked after until they could be reunited with their families.

I was accepted for this program and on June 5, 1939 went to England on a Kindertransport. I had to be at the railway station early one morning with one suitcase. Only one parent was allowed to accompany me. Our goodbyes had to be said inside the waiting room, not on the platform.

We climbed into the carriage and, being the oldest at 13, I was put in charge. Most of the children were quite young but everything happened so quickly there was no time to cry.

The train started and off we went. No waving goodbye as the windows were closed. No seeing our parents for the last time, no nothing.

Our first stop was just over the border in Holland. People standing on the platform handed us drinks and sandwiches, cakes and sweets. They even had little toys for the youngest children some of whom were only 4 years old.

The train traveled on to a harbor. We all embarked on a ferry where we were four to a cabin. I found this quite exciting as I had never seen the sea before. In the morning, we docked in Harwich, England and were driven by bus to a huge hall. I was happy to see all our suitcases waiting for us under alphabetical signs.

Identification cards were hung around our necks with our names and destinations noted. Most of us were put on a train to London's Liverpool Street Station. We were met by the Ladies of the Jewish Relief Committee for Refugees. One of the first things I noticed was that some of the women had fingernails painted red. I had never seen that before. These women took us to another large hall opposite the station where long tables had been set up laden with food, drinks and other tasty snacks.

After lunch, we were divided into small groups, and those of us who already had destinations were issued additional tabs around our necks listing our new address. Three of us were driven to Kings Cross Station to board a train called the "Flying Scotsman." Our stop was to be Newcastle in the North of England. We were given 10 shillings each and settled on seats in the dining car.

The people around us were very kind and kept getting us drinks and sandwiches during the 6-hour journey. Of course, our communication was all done with sign language, and it was on this trip that I learned my first English word: Refugee. We were all given lots of good wishes and thumbs-up signs when we got off the train.

One of the ladies of the Sunderland Refugee Girls Hostel Committee met our train and took us to our new home. We were welcomed by the Matron, formerly of Vienna, the cook, who was a former cook for a Jewish Old Folks home in Hamburg, two maids, who were local girls, and the 18 girls already living there. In all there were 28 of us.

The middle of three large red-brick Victorian buildings, each three stories high, was our home. All of the very large rooms had a fireplace. Because it was cold in the summer and freezing in winter, these fireplaces were well used. Of the other two buildings, one was still privately owned, while the third one became a rehabilitation center for wounded soldiers after the war started.

Downstairs, we had three reception rooms, two kitchens—each one with a coal-fired range, like the ones in old films, a pantry, which used to be the domain of the butler, and a bathroom. In the large yard at the back were a washhouse with a coal-fired range for boiling the clothes, a hand-operated mangle, and four pulleys for hanging the washing to dry.

The first floor had five bedrooms, two toilets, two cubicles with bathtubs and four sinks. The second floor had four bedrooms and conveniences. Under the roof were four small rooms for the staff. The beds, blankets, bedding and towels were all brand new as were all the kitchen utensils. The Jews in Sunderland dealt in furniture, textiles and fashion, so I guess they had donated everything for the hostel. We settled in fairly well, but after lights out I remember hearing a lot of crying.

We immediately began going to the local school, but it was soon realized that we had to learn English first. Every day a retired school teacher, Miss Robinson, came to teach English to us. We were divided into three groups. She was patient and kind, and I still remember her with great affection.

There were two synagogues in Sunderland and we went to them on Saturdays alternating between the two. We walked in a crocodile formation and were not allowed to speak German in the street.

We were often invited to tea, to the cinema and the Pantomime by various well wishers. But for us, the best times of the day were the twice daily postal deliveries. Day by day, during July and August 1939, fewer and fewer letters arrived.

At 11 a.m. on September 3rd, we sat around the radio to hear a man named Chamberlain make a speech. Though we could not understand what he said, we soon learned that England had declared war on Germany. Now we children were on one side while our families were trapped on the other side. Fortunately, my parents and brother managed to reach England the week before the war began. Only one other girl and I were this lucky. All the rest of the children lost their families. After Chamberlain's speech, we heard the air raid siren for the first time. It was very scary.

Everything changed dramatically after September 3rd. Sunderland is a coastal town as well as a large ship building center. It was declared a closed area for foreigners over 16 years of age. Our matron and cook had to leave town. The maids had to do war work. We, especially the older kids, had to do the work in the house and kitchen. Our new matron was Irish, was not able to communicate with us, and was a dreadful cook.

It was a really terrible time for us girls. The nightly air raids never let up. Night after night, we had to go into the cellar, carrying our gas masks and photos. We were frightened, and we shivered there sometimes for hours until the all clear sounded.

In August 1942, I joined my parents in London. My father had been interned and my mother and brother evacuated to the countryside. It was after the Blitzkrieg (the German bombardment of London) in 1940. My father got a job as a bookkeeper and my mother a job sewing. We lived in two small rented rooms with kitchen facilities and a shared bathroom.

London was in a sorry state. The docks and city were in ruins. Most streets had empty spaces where houses had been destroyed by the bombs. The windows that had been left were taped and the rest covered with boards. The buses had wire netting taped to the glass and there was a complete blackout nightly. You could be fired from your job if even a tiny chink of light showed from any of your windows.

We still had air raids except when there was a full moon. All along the platforms in the London Underground stations two-tier bunks had been built. Whole families spent their nights here. Shelters were built along streets and in people's gardens. The safest place in a house during an air raid was deemed to be the cubbyhole under the stairs.

I obtained a job as an apprentice dressmaker in a salon in Grosvenor Square opposite the American Embassy. My duties included making tea, picking up precious pins, following the director upstairs carrying garments and being a general "dogsbody". In between these tasks, I learned to be a real dressmaker. I must say that I still benefit from that training up to this day.

When there was an air raid, we all crawled under the cutting table. Despite air raids, ration books, clothing coupons, shortages of absolutely everything we still had fun. There were cinemas, dances, theaters and soldiers. London was awash with servicemen and servicewomen from all over the world.

I was issued an "Alien Identity Card" upon my 16th birthday. I had to carry this card with me at all times.

In late 1943, the Germans began sending a new destructive device over London. It was called the flying bomb. When one was approaching, you heard a steady droning sound. The point where the noise stopped was where the bomb would fall. There was really no escaping. If it got you, that was it.

Once again, there was an evacuation program. My mother and brother were sent to a small country village while I remained in London with my father. Being young, I got used to the interruption of these flying bombs, and come what may, I still managed to have fun.

We had no news of what was happening to the Jews in Europe. When the Allies returned to fight on European soil, it gave us a glimmer of hope for a victorious end to the war. But there was one more attempt to scare the British population into surrender. Called the V2 Rocket, it was a terrifying device. No droning sound from the V2. It just suddenly exploded on the ground and that was it.

Beginning in 1945, it became clear that the Allies would win the war. I had changed my job and was now a full-fledged dressmaker. We had moved to a larger apartment, and rationing had been somewhat eased.

After I heard what had happened in Europe, I realized how lucky I had been to be on the Kindertransport that 5th of June 1939.

Daisy's
Photo
Album

Berlin
Marienbad
Ra'anana, Israel

My parents Ettel and
Samson Rubin, Berlin 1935.

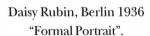

Daisy Rubin, Berlin 1936
"Formal Portrait".

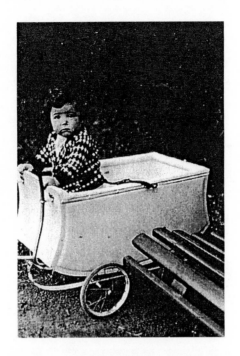

"Bobby" in his pram, Tiergarten, Berlin.

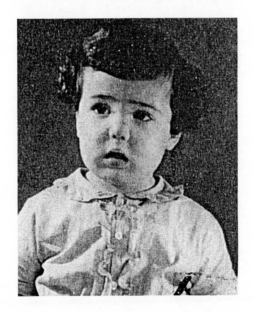

My brother Lion (Bobby), Berlin 1938.

With my parents in Marienbad, Czechoslovakia.

Adass Yisroel Lyceum, Berlin 1939. Daisy is third girl from left, next to Dr. Rebhun. Ellen is center front.

My father Samson Rubin, Berlin 1936.

One of my father's creations. A sample of
Hebrew calligraphy.

Daisy, Ra'anana, Israel.

Daisy with her four great grandchildren. Shira,
Shachar, Noa and Sohar. Ra'anana, Israel 2004.

Daisy at her home, Ra'anana, 2004, Israel.

Daisy with Mendel Roessler, her husband. Israel.

Epilogue

There are moments in people's lives that, although they may not realize it at the time, will make a difference between life and death, joy and sadness, captivity and freedom. I want to tell you about two such moments in the life of my own family.

Four years ago I came across a book review about Major Frank Foley who was working as an agent at the British Embassy in Berlin during the 1930s. What caught my eye in that article was that he had helped thousands of Jews escape from Germany. He had issued thousands of transit visas to Palestine, then under British Mandate, that enabled Jews to leave, and thus saved their lives.

My father had written to relatives and friends all over the world asking for help to get his family out of Germany. I had been sent to England on the Kindertransport in June 1939, but Dad, Mum and my little brother had nowhere to go. My father had to leave his job as Office Manager at the end of 1938 as his place of work had been "Aryanized."

The General Manager of "ERKO, GmbH" was Major Rudolf von Oersten, retired. He had joined the S.A. (Nazi Party) and thus he was now head of the firm. He and my father had always been good friends and he had warned my Dad not to sleep at home on November 9, 1938, the night of "Kristallnacht." Unbeknown to my father, he had also written to a business friend in London asking him to help with a British Visa for my father.

In July 1939 Dad received a letter from the British Embassy that a Six-Month Visa was to be issued to him and he was to present himself at a side door of the embassy. In those days hundreds of people stood in line outside foreign embassies for days on end hoping to acquire a transit visa to leave Germany. Dad went as instructed and he did not have to wait in line.

When Dad presented his passport to the clerk at the embassy, he was asked if he had a family. "Yes," he replied, "I have a wife, a two-year old son, and a daughter who is now in England."

"Does your wife have a passport?"

"Yes. Actually, I have it with me. My son will be two at the end of the month, so I had to add his name to my wife's passport."

"May I see it?"

My father handed the second passport to the clerk who then asked him to wait. Soon the passports were returned to him and when he got home my parents saw that both passports had been stamped with a visa. They were even "work visas".

To the end of his days, my father thought that the clerk had made a mistake! But they left Berlin together just before September 3, 1939 when the war began, and arrived in London via Holland.

Now, after 60 years, I know the name of the person who saved the lives of my Mum and my brother Bobby.

In March 2004 I was looking at old photos and glanced through my "Poesie Album". I had packed the album into my one little suitcase when I left Berlin on June 5, 1939. All my friends and teachers had written little verses and good wishes in this book. As I looked at the names, I wondered what had happened to these friends. Were they alive or were they dead? I had kept in touch with two girls all these years and I decided then and there to try and find out if any others were still around.

I wrote to the *Berliner-Burgermeister* (Mayor of Berlin) listing the girls' names and the schools we had attended, my old Berlin address, and asked if he could help. Three weeks later I received an answer. My letter would be published in the twice yearly *Aktuell Magazine* that is sent worldwide to old Berlin residents.

In June 2004 letters and phone calls started to come in. It was wonderful! I found four classmates, three of them living in Israel. I have visited them all and after 65 years we talked as though we had parted only yesterday!

But there was one letter that brought grief and sadness. This letter was sent by a man in Germany. He was a retired librarian and, when he saw my letter with the names, he decided to investigate. It seems there is a book listing Berliners who had been sent to extermination camps.

Nine names on that list coincided with those of my friends. I knew that our class teacher Dr. David Rebhun had perished, and now I know also that at least nine old school friends suffered the same fate.

I have inscribed their names in the computerized list for Holocaust victims. I am glad I wrote that letter. This one deed has brought me much joy as well as great sadness.

Daisy Rubin Roessler . Israel . 2005

Lisa Klein

Biography

For Lisa Klein, born 1925 in Berlin, 1939 was a most exciting year. She was sent with the "Kindertransport (Children's Transport)" to London where her family joined her a few months later when they sailed via Ellis Island to the Dominican Republic. After seven years there, she left, again alone, for New York City. Lisa has lived on her own most of her life. She worked as secretary in non-profit, big business and legal offices. She finished her education going to night school, first in Washington Heights High School, then finished City College with a B.A degree. She has enjoyed all her jobs that have enabled her to travel many times to Europe to visit the few relatives who survived Hitler's gruesome regime. Lisa has many good friends, loves New York City where she lives on the upper West Side. She has also visited several times the unforgettable canyons and wonders in the western part of the USA. She feels this is a great country, however, there is some part of her that remains European. Her motto is: *To Live and Let Live.*

Lisa Klein - CONTENTS

Childhood Memories In Hitler's Third Reich

Living in Berlin during the 1930s

We were a family of four: father, mother, an older brother and I. We were middle class. Father had a good position as an account executive for a technical journal of textile manufacturers titled *The Konfektionaer*. Father traveled at least twice a month to the textile manufacturing towns Leipzig and Chemnitz, in eastern Germany. Mother (called Mutti) didn't work but had many friends and loved playing bridge. We children had a nurse, later a governess, and always a cook who stayed with us for a long time. Our parents left us children pretty much alone with the governess. They would spend their winter vacation without us, but during the summer vacation, we all went to visit Mother's sister, Tante (Aunt) Irma, and her family of three children in Norderney, an island in the North Sea.

Books

Our apartment in Berlin was very comfortable. My father had a fairly large study with a big oak desk, a beautiful, round, standing pipe stove to heat the room with wood in the winter, and a large library. Many books were lined up in a big glass cabinet under lock and key. When I was 7 or 8, I was consumed with reading. I read all the children's books in our children's bedroom and then learned where Mutti had hidden the key to the large library. (In those days there was concern that a young child would be much influenced by a book and therefore adults were strict about what one could read.) I read what my hands could reach—often on subjects I didn't understand—but no matter, all got read, even "Sappho", which, of course, I didn't have any idea what it was all about.

My favorite cousin Gisela, who was 8 years older than I, had the first Tarzan volume by Edgar Rice Burroughs. I devoured it and then could hardly sleep. How to get the other volumes! I got myself a Public Library card and looked for Vol. II there. When I found it, the Librarian looked at me sternly and said, "That's not for children. Does your mother know you are getting this book?" Of course I lied and she let me have it.

Mother would often take me with her when visiting her bridge partners. One of her friends had two boys and would let me go to the boys' room filled with adventure books. I was in heaven! I read Karl May's books on the Red Indians in America, Winnetou, the courageous and gentle Red Indian Chief, and Old Shatterhand, the English gentleman who made friends with Winnetou. Besides these series, Karl May also wrote about sandy Africa and the Muslims' adventures. I could feel the heat and dryness there and sympathized with the African friend. Karl May wrote these in jail, by the way. I also read Zane Gray about life and wolves on icy North Pole, Jack London, Edgar Wallace, "Robinson Crusoe", all in German of course. But Tarzan still was the best! My mother found out about my reading from my Aunt Irma (Mother's oldest sister) who had moved to Berlin in the 1930's. I slept over there every now and then and would read with a flashlight under my sheet into the middle of the night. Mutti was not too pleased—but that didn't stop me.

Movies

The big film industry was created by the "UFA." Going to the movies became very fashionable. Mutti loved the movies but, alas, children under 15 were not allowed to most of them. (Not at all like in the USA where many children went to see adventure movies Saturday afternoons.) When "King Kong" came over from the USA, it was a sensation. Mutti was determined to see it, but what to do with me? I begged her to take me along. So I wore her high-heel shoes, she put up my hair, used lipstick on me, made me wear the longest dress I had and tried to smuggle me in—it didn't work. The UFA became the mouthpiece for the Nazi propaganda and of course we didn't go anymore to the movies.

Our lives change

Even though our parents didn't speak much about politics to my brother or me, we sensed that changes were occurring. We noticed the proliferation of men in uniforms everywhere. Troops marched the streets in their black boots, brown uniforms with wide red bands around their upper arms showing a "Hakenkreuz" (Swastika) on a white round background, and raising their arms with the "Heil Hitler" salute. Many children's groups—the "Hitlerjugend" (Hitler youth) of very young teenagers, and the girls' BDM groups ("Bund Deutscher Maedchen"—the League of German Girls)—paraded proudly with their Swastika flags, all singing anti-Semitic songs. Most frightening to us was the anti-Semitic Horst Wessel song "Die Fahne hoch" (Lift the Banner High) and "Wenn das Judenblut vom Messer spritzt" ("When Jewish blood drips from our knives.")

At first, my brother and I wanted to join these groups. They sounded so patriotic. We wanted to be part of these seemingly friendly leagues. But we soon understood that we could not be part of this because we were "the enemy" and were excluded.

When I saw one of the early Nazi films (about 1935), titled "Hitlerjunge Quex," it made me cry because it depicted a fine, young, upright, blue-eyed, golden haired boy, who had to courageously fight the bad Communist and Socialist youths who attacked him in the streets. (In reality it was the Nazis who attacked the Communist and Socialist groups.) It was a very clever, impressive and moving film. I only vaguely recall the film now, but I do remember the emotional impact it had on me. Only when my mother explained to me that this film was pure emotional propaganda for the Nazi Party, did I calm down. But then I got frightened!

My father was a stern man. Although he traveled much and had many journalist friends, he couldn't believe their warnings of what was to come. Some of these friends had read Hitler's book, *Mein Kampf* (My Struggle), but Father had not. When the Nazis were fighting the Socialists and Communists in the streets during the late 1920s and early 1930s, he was unconcerned. When Hitler and the Nazis became more powerful, he said, "The Nazis can't possibly win." When Hitler finally became Chancellor in January 1933 and only one month later had the Reichstag (German Parliament) burnt down, Father said, "Hitler can't last. The German people won't let it happen." Even after the first anti-Semitic laws were published, he still held on to his optimism, saying he had his "Iron Cross" that had been awarded him for his military service in World War I, as it had to so many other Jewish men. He pulled a velvet box out of his writing desk drawer and proudly showed the Iron Cross to us. It was the first and only time I ever saw it. When he lost his job in 1936, he began to understand the danger to the entire Jewish population.

Around this time the sign "Juden Verboten" (Jews not allowed) appeared all over Berlin—at my favorite swimming pool, in many restaurants, stores, and public places. My favorite public school teacher announced one day that all Jews must sit in the back rows of the classroom. We were only 8 Jewish children in a class of 38 girls. Most of us had been sitting up front where the better students sat—a German school rule at that time. We were all stunned. Even our teacher was embarrassed.

Then a few weeks later, another blow. I was a very good gymnast and always participated in the "Parents Evening" at the end of each semester. I was told I could not participate anymore. I cried. I was an outcast. A few months later, a further blow! My teacher came walking down our street and my face lit up because I liked him so much. To my great amazement, though his face flushed visibly, he looked away without greeting me! And I had been his favorite student— once upon a time! I still feel the hurt!

To my knowledge, the anti-Semitism and the violent Nazi behavior were not as evident in Berlin. It was, after all, a great metropolitan and cosmopolitan city, where so many foreign visitors came to see the 1936 Olympics. Anti-Jewish behavior was restrained. My parents shielded us children from what was happening as much as they could. There were seldom any discussions in front of us, but, of course, we felt the tension, particularly after my father lost his job.

One day, when I was walking home from school under the beautiful chestnut trees along the Uferstrasse next to the Spree—the small river wending through Berlin—two boys suddenly appeared. They were about my age (11), and yelled anti-Semitic slogans at me. I was both surprised and frightened. Nobody came to my rescue when they tried to beat me with long carton tubes. I pulled myself together, sprinted along the street and outran them. Little did they know I was the best runner in school! Yet, the event left me quite shaken.

In 1936, all Jewish children had to switch to Jewish schools. I entered the Adass Jisroel, a Lyzeum (high school) for girls in Siegmundshof Strasse. A rabbi, Dr. Rebhuhn, was our class teacher. My parents were neither orthodox nor did they keep to the kosher laws. We went to synagogue only on the High Holidays. So, it was a surprise to me to have a rabbi as teacher, even though my parents had sent me to private Hebrew classes given by a rabbi, on Sundays, during the last year in Public School. They wanted me to learn more about our Jewish religion including some Hebrew. However, going to the Adass Jisroel school became chaotic because every one of us Jews was trying to leave Germany. From day-to-day we had different teachers. Years later I learned that Rabbi Rebhuhn never made it out of Germany and perished in Auschwitz.

There were a number of well-known Jewish lyceums in Berlin and they decided to hold a Jewish Sports event. I was a good athlete and ran well and fast. So I was entered as 50-meter runner for the Adass Jisroel school. And I won! A great triumph—except that when they celebrated the victory, I had to stay home with an appendicitis attack and missed the ceremonies.

At home, with Father around all the time, things were difficult. Mutti finally decided to become more forceful and insisted that we all learn English. Mother had four sisters. One sister, Auntie Heddy, had married a well-to-do English Jewish businessman and lived in London. Mutti had visited them in 1914 where she had been caught by World War I and so had to remain in England where she learned English. We children were eager to learn a new language. We'd gather at the round oak table in the dining room with its big windows facing the street. Our two caged canaries usually sang their song, while we repeated English words. Mutti had bought the *1000 Woerter in Englisch* (One Thousand Words in English), a ten-volume book and very handy because each volume contained five lessons, was thin and simple. I even remember the first sentence in Vol. 1: "How do you do, Mr. Smith?"

Mother had three sisters and one adopted cousin. One lived in London, Auntie Heddy, one in Koenigsberg (then still in Germany, now Kaliningrad, Russia), and later in Berlin, Tante Irma, and one in Czechoslovakia, Tante Else. The adopted cousin immigrated with husband and one child to Argentina earlier, perhaps in 1937. Tante Else's beloved husband suddenly died in Czechoslovakia in 1938. They had no children. Heart-broken and alone, she decided to join her sister in London and thus escape persecution by the Nazis. She told Auntie Heddy of the atrocities of the Nazi regime and the rumored concentration camps and the new anti-Semitic Nazi laws in Germany and Austria. The English family didn't really realize the danger to the Jews. It was upon the insistence of my Tante Else that they finally tried to get visas for my family of 4 (mother, father, brother and I) and Tante Irma's family of 5 (she, her husband, a daughter and two sons) to immigrate to England. By now, England gave out only transit visas but it saved the lives of two families, 9 people altogether.

November 9, 1938, "Kristallnacht"! Rumors spread that the Nazis were rounding up Jewish men and youths. The family decided my father and brother should stay overnight with his sister-in-law who lived alone with her two daughters nearby. Mutti and I huddled together in the front entrance room all morning and afternoon, shivering with fear. Then a knock came at the door in early evening. Mutti and I were holding hands when she opened the door. Two men in suits, Gestapo!, asked, "Is the man of the house at home?" Mutti answered "No" in a shaky voice, and, to our surprise, the two men shrugged their shoulders and left without searching the apartment. We were very lucky. The next day we learned that many Jewish men had been taken, including some of our friends and their older sons. These men were pushed into vans. Some were taken to Gestapo Headquarters while others were transported out of Berlin.

It was a terrible time for all Jews. We hardly dared to go out anymore. I no longer went to school. We tried to prepare for emigration. My brother was sent as an apprentice to a dye factory to learn a trade. Mutti took up millinery. Father spent many hours daily trying to get forms, documents and visas from foreign consulates to emigrate anywhere—without success. He started with Australia, Switzerland, then Portugal, Mexico, Argentina and finally Uruguay. Every rumor of visas being issued was followed up.

My parents started to sell items not needed for emigration. I remember the man who came to buy our silver. It was in a beautiful red velvet box and he seemed very pleased with the spoons and knives but, alas, they had our initials on them. He was willing to pay us for the silver and my parents needed money to emigrate. What to do! The man finally took pity on us and said he could possibly remove the initials. He paid a little less and took the heavy box on his shoulder, warned us not to tell anybody about this, and left.

My father was also able to sell his stamp collection. I remember helping him collect stamps. He would send me, by myself, to foreign consulates in our neighborhood where I'd knock on the door and ask for stamps. I learned to wash and clean the stamps before putting them into the stamp book. So I was sorry that this occasion to be my father's pet was coming to an end. Jews were not allowed to sell anything nor to buy money, so we were taking a chance on selling any items. I'm glad that Mutti managed to pack some of our porcelain. I still have a porcelain bowl, white with blue crowns and golden handle, that I treasure.

Now, my parents started frantically getting ready to leave. I did not fully understand how they must have felt dissolving a seven-room household, abandoning their comfortable apartment, their comfortable lives, and not knowing the future—or even if they had a future. I was then living only in my world. However, I do remember the huge crates standing in the courtyard with loads of boxes packed with linen, chinaware, a sewing machine, kitchen utensils, clothing, and some—but not all—of our paintings and Oriental rugs.

Every few weeks these crates were re-stenciled with our latest destination. The stencils started with O'Porto in Portugal, Mexico City, then Montevideo in Urugay, and so on. Many hopeful Jewish emigrants put their belongings in crates called "lifts" and sent them to Hamburg warehouses with the intention to have these lifts forwarded to wherever they were able to immigrate. Mutti preferred to take our crates with us whenever we moved. One day we heard that the Nazis had burned down the warehouses in Hamburg and many people lost their lifts.

The day we received permission to leave Germany for England, two Gestapo men were stationed in our apartment to oversee the packing. We were forbidden to take any gold or silver articles, anything of value plus other restrictions. Word had it that these men like to drink. So my parents bought a case of bottled beer and kept the two men supplied while packing. After many beers, they became very sleepy thus making it possible for Mutti to slip in a few valuable items. She was just packing her favorite silver sugar bowl when one of the men opened his eyes and commanded, "Stop!" She did. The Gestapo man shook his partner awake and said in a slurred voice, "Isn't that bowl made of silver?" Angry at being awakened, the other man, in a grumpy voice, said, "How do I know?" and promptly fell asleep again. The first man turned to Mutti and asked, "Is that bowl made of silver?" Mutti coolly replied "No," and he let her pack it.

After the Kristallnacht, my parents heard of the agreement reached by the British Government and the Jewish agencies in London and Berlin with the Hitler regime to let Jewish children, ages 5 to 16, go to England. Little did the Nazis know how generous the English were or that this agreement would save about 10,000 Jewish children. Right away my father went to the Juedische Gemeinde (Jewish Agency) in Berlin to put my name on the "Kindertransport" (Children transport) list. My brother could not go because he was over 16.

By March 1939 I still had not been called. We found out that my name had gotten lost. But then finally, on June 5, 1939 my day came. We children were allowed one small suitcase and given a list of things we could pack. Suddenly there I was, standing on the platform in the Hauptbahnhof (main railroad station) in Berlin, surrounded by many weeping children and parents hugging and kissing and crying. I then climbed onto the train with 60 to 100 other children. (I don't remember crying; yet I weep now while writing this, and I cry when someone leaves me.) Soon the train lurched, and we all started off into an unknown future. I was one of the lucky ones. I had family in London!

To my shame, I must admit that before boarding the train in Berlin, one of the older assistants asked if I would agree to take care of two little children, age 5, during the journey. I became quite angry at being asked to do this and haughtily refused. It wasn't only that I felt put upon, but that I had never taken care of anyone else. My brother did for me but never I for him. This refusal still haunts me!

We were told to be very quiet and to sit still as long as the train was in Germany. We were also directed to be courteous to inspectors boarding the train and never to open a window. All of us were pretty apprehensive; so were our escorts. A few inspectors did come around to ask questions and inspect some of the suitcases at the border. But then we were in Holland! A great "Hurrah!" erupted from all of us. We immediately opened the windows and yelled and laughed. Soon we pulled into a Dutch station where a number of elderly, grey-haired ladies, were waving at us as the train stopped. They handed out chocolates and even let us jump off the train to run around in a nearby meadow to stretch our legs. We all cried with relief and were overcome by this hospitality.

The train ride continued with some very happy children. In Hoek van Holland, we boarded a ship that would ferry us across the English Channel to Harwich in England. The channel was choppy that night and some of the children got seasick. I slept through the whole trip. In Harwich, we climbed aboard another train, which took us to Liverpool Street Station in London. We all were glad to have finally arrived after our exhausting journey.

My favorite Aunt Else, who had just left Czechoslovakia to live in London, came to pick me up at Liverpool Street Station. She explained to me that my English Aunt Heddy didn't have room for me in her house, and that I would go to a "hostel" where other refugee children stayed temporarily. And so I ended up near Kensington Gardens in a small private hostel for children, which was under the auspices of the Bloomsbury House or Woburn House, a Jewish Agency, also probably supported by the English Government. I was not homesick. I fitted into this setup quite happily. It was as though I was on a great adventure—and so it was. Except for the three-week evacuation to the countryside when World War II started, I lived in that hostel four months. At that point, my family and I emigrated to the Dominican Republic.

In London 1939

When I think of England, I always smile! How can I ever forget the generosity of the English people and how they saved almost 10,000 mainly Jewish children from death by the Nazis. About 200 such transports were made from December 1, 1938 to the end of August 1939. Planning the exodus of so many children, their distribution in England, and organizing this program in such a short time, had to have been a tremendous undertaking.

These children were coming in droves from Germany, Austria, Czechoslovakia and some from Poland. All were saved by the" Kindertransport" arrangement between the British Parliament (ex-Prime Minister Baldwin, I believe, was very much involved), the Jewish Agencies in London and Berlin and the German Government. Most of the trains left from Berlin and Vienna, I believe. This small island of England offered a new home and security to so many of us while a big country like the USA did not.

On June 6, 1939 I stepped on English soil. My favorite Aunt Elsie (Mother's third sister) took me directly by cab from Liverpool Station to my new abode, a "hostel" in Lexington Gardens. It was not far from the beautiful Kensington Gardens park. In this hostel we were 12 to 18 children, 5 to 16 years of age, boys and girls. I was not sorry that my two aunts in London (Aunt Else from Czechoslovakia, and Auntie Heddy who lived in London) could not put me up because I preferred to be with children of my own age. "I spent the best and most wonderful time in this hostel," I once wrote.

I understood at that time that three such hostels were hired and run by the Woburn House (or Bloomsbury House) the Jewish Agency in London, to accommodate at least some of us Jewish children who, almost daily, were arriving mostly from Germany and Austria. It was a long trip for young children. They left by train, then sailed by boat across the choppy English Channel, and again traveled by train to London. At that time I had no idea that there were so many of us.

In Germany, many families received English newspapers through the Jewish Agencies and answered ads for domestic help or farm workers or whatever. Desperate to find a home for their children, as well as themselves, they pleaded for acceptance of their child with the promise of domestic help. Others wrote to well-known wealthy Jewish families to accept their child. One of those wealthy families was the Rothschilds who accepted a number of children (I believe about 25) and let them live on their grounds.

It was a terribly trying time, a terribly frightening time, and a very hopeless time. We children were not so much aware of it. Almost every day at least one child would leave for a new home, a new family, a new situation and new children would arrive. I was the only child who stayed in the hostel as long as I was in London. The older children found work as domestics or farm laborers with people who were located by the Woburn or Bloomsbury House. It was not an easy task to find homes for so many children—yet it was done! Not every one was happily domiciled. Some had bad experiences and some children returned to the hostel—but by and large, of the many "Kinder" I met throughout the years, most had found a loving home. And some who had bad experiences were able to change their situation with the help of the Woburn House.

In my hostel we had an elderly English landlady who didn't speak German, cooked the English way and tried to keep the house clean. She was overwhelmed with the task of keeping order in this medley of young children who didn't speak English, were lost and scared and had never had such liberty! We children very quickly found out that she had no idea how to manage us. We got bored and did not like her very much nor the food she prepared. So there was trouble!

The Woburn House heard about this and sent a governess to take over. Her name was Miss Ruth Ehrmann, from Germany. She was small, stout and highly intelligent. She took charge immediately and our lives changed. At first we hated her and tried to rebel but when she said, "You won't get any supper if you don't obey," we gave in. She made plans for every day listing what the girls had to do to help our landlady: laying the table, washing laundry, ironing, mending stockings, sewing. The boys also had to do their laundry and other tasks. She arranged storytelling evenings, radio music hour after supper, mainly classical, (I loved

Beethoven and would close my eyes to listen), and she would tell us about her life. We soon loved her.

She also took us on wonderful trips to see and understand more of London and the country that had saved our lives. These trips took us all over, to Hyde Park, the Houses of Parliament, 10 Downing Street, Westminster Abbey, Trafalgar Square, Scotland Yard, Piccadilly Circus, Oxford Street, Marble Arch, the Albert Memorial, The Tower, and the famous museums such as the Tate Gallery, the British Museum, the National Gallery. Miss Ehrmann also gave us daily English lessons. We were so busy. She enriched our lives in a way I can never forget. She was a true pediatric educator.

(Much much later I found out she became a child psychologist, married, lived in Chile, and had a daughter. She wrote an interesting book on her professional experience in Chile as a psychologist and I found a copy of that book. She died in Chile.)

After a number of weeks, I got the happy news that my parents and brother were coming to London. My brother was sent to my hostel and my parents stayed in my cousin's house (my Aunt Heddy's oldest daughter) in Golders Green. I continued to live in the hostel and enjoyed every moment of it, even though I fell madly in love with a 16-year old boy who tried to commit suicide!

I became friends with a girl my age called Leah. We slept in the same room, and we had many laughs together. We laughed so much one night that Miss Ehrmann pulled us out of our beds and made us sleep on the stairs! But after a half-hour, when we were in tears, she allowed us to go back to bed. We had learned our lesson!

One day the boys played warriors in the basement and sprayed water all over themselves and the floor. Everything was swimming—the laundry, the dirt, dead spiders, old lumber. Well, Miss Ehrmann came and punished them—no dinner, but she also understood that the boys were protesting about having to do their laundry. So we girls were assigned to wash the boys' laundry from then on. We girls were not delighted.

Our landlady tried to cook for us but we were accustomed to different meals. Almost every morning she served hot porridge. We didn't know this cereal and nobody wanted to eat it except one person—me. So, the girls would give me their portion and I would line each plate up in front of me and happily devour one after the other. Every evening we got cocoa (chocolate milk) with bread and sometimes cheese or sardines. Miss Ehrmann complained to the Woburn House. One day a lady representative of the Woburn House entered just as we were having cocoa with bread and butter and nothing else. She was astonished when she found out that this was our usual supper. She gave some money to Miss Ehrmann for the children to go to the movies. She also had a cousin who had a farm send us lots of fruits, as well as sweets and chocolate, and discussed food with the landlady.

On another day, we were just playing Ping-Pong, an English woman, poorly dressed, came in. She said she was a washerwoman and asked if this was the house where the poor refugees were living. We first didn't understand her accent. Then the landlady came and said: "This lady is giving you a box full of chocolates. She wishes to help you. Instead of going on a holiday, she prefers to make all of you happy!"

I had dinner once a week in Auntie Heddy's beautiful house, in Hampstead Heath, with her two daughters, husband and my Aunt Else from Czechoslovakia. Auntie Else also showed me London and took me to the movies, where, to my astonishment, they served cold drinks and sweets during intermission. I grew very fond of my two aunts.

When my parents finally arrived in London mid-August, and also Aunt Irma's family, we were all much relieved but still needed to find another country to immigrate to. The English Government only issued a 6-month transit visa for my parents! Perhaps they would have let us stay, because the war started in the meantime, but my father and my English aunt were trying very hard to find another country.

As the end of August approached, the political situation grew more and more grave. War between Nazi Germany and England seemed inevitable. Hitler threatened Poland despite Prime Minister Chamberlain's appeasement policy which resulted in Hitler's takeover of Czechoslovakia. Every day, every hour, war could break out. London was as quiet as always though changes were visible. Air raid shelters were built. In front of every official building sandbags were towered up and policemen were standing at every corner. Gas masks were distributed. Everybody had to carry one. Soon they became fashionable and gas mask boxes were sold to fit to the color of the dress. It looked as if the ladies were carrying hatboxes.

Blackout exercises began. The first one was frightening. The hostel was in a district with tall houses. (At that time 4-6 floors were considered high.) At night, everybody had to switch off the lights or else put dark paper over the windows. We had no dark paper and therefore only darkness in the house. All you could see was a street wrapped in mist and obscurity. The houses seemed like great ghostly giants. I became afraid, looked for my girlfriend and we both held on to each other and shivered together.

Every day we still had new children coming and others leaving. One day a new girl came. She was very tall but only 12 years old. We called her the "Baby Elephant." We liked her very much. Two weeks later, on the 29th of August, she left to meet her mother in Antwerp, Belgium, then to proceed to the Dominican Republic to which her father had immigrated. At that time I had no idea where this country was, had never heard of it. She went away quite alone. She wore three ribbons, blue, red and white, around each arm. These ribbons identified her at the various stations she had to travel through to get to Belgium. At every station one person from the Jewish Committee was to meet her and direct her on to the next station.

On August 30th Miss Ehrmann informed us that all children living near Buckingham Palace and Hyde Park Corner were going to be evacuated. In our hostel, girls were being sent to a camp in Tunbridge Wells and the boys to a camp in Ipswich. All of us were very excited. Another adventure!

We took leave of the house where we had lived happily, frightened and also contentedly. When we got to the railroad station, we saw hundreds of children departing for new homes as well as soldiers leaving their old homes, all going away from London, the one to be saved and the other to uncertainty and perhaps death. From that train we saw the blockade of balloons (called barrage balloons), hundreds of them, to prevent German planes to get to London and drop their bombs.

We arrived in Tunbridge Wells after a three-hour train ride. We were all happy to be safe but our walk to our new home through this little town where all its residents came out to stare at us foreigners was a little unnerving. Then we were in for a surprise: instead of the camp we'd expected, we saw a castle! It was a wonderful mansion, surrounded by parks and meadows. All of us were delighted. We were told that an English countess had given this mansion as an evacuation camp for girls.

We were about 60 young girls altogether and all had to pitch in with the cleaning of rooms and particularly the kitchen. The beautiful park tempted me to climb a tree but wisely I didn't. We were kept very busy once Miss Ehrmann arrived three days later. We were given pocket money every two weeks, and once were allowed to go to the movies, a special treat in those days. We heard from the boys who were sent to Ipswich. They were not as happy as we were because they had to work very hard and were not living in a mansion.

A few days later, a new arrival—it was our Baby Elephant, Gerda. She was in tears. When she arrived in Southampton to go by boat to Belgium to meet her mother, the war broke out. The ship did not sail, nor was her mother allowed to leave Germany. Gerda had to return to Dover to a relative, then back to London to our hostel, found out we had been evacuated, and finally reached us, tired, alone and sad.

September 1, 1939, Hitler attacked Poland with planes and soldiers. September 3, England declared war! As young as we were, we knew this was serious. Luckily we were fairly safe. We were sent to town to fetch gas masks. I now had two, one from London and from Tunbridge Wells.

About 6 a.m., a few days later, we heard the air raid sirens. Our first air raid! We sprang out of our beds and then were told to go to the garage with our gas masks on. We didn't feel safe in this garage hearing the airplanes buzzing above us, and we waited and waited—it seemed a lifetime. We thought the planes we heard were the Germans, the sirens we heard were the British Air Force (the R.A.F.) catching the Germans. Finally we had to take off the gas masks because we couldn't breathe anymore. They were so hot. After more than two hours, we heard voices outside and found out that the air raid was over two hours ago—it had merely been an exercise.

About two weeks later, my parents wrote that soon we would sail off to Buenos Aires, so I went back to London to stay with my parents in my cousin's house. Up to now the Blitzkrieg had not yet started. We lived a fairly normal life. My brother and the youngest son of Tante Irma came back from Ipswich. Two families survived because of my English aunt! I don't remember where Tante Irma lived but their youngest son stayed with us.

In the meantime, Auntie Heddy with my father got the runaround from the Argentinean Consul and the Dominican Consul, each one telling her she had to first get the other's permission for a visa. Was it distrust or prejudice or bureaucracy? It seemed we had to get a ship to Santo Domingo and from there on to Argentina. My aunt then made an arrangement with a man recommended to her who dealt with these situations. She paid him a lot of money. My father warned her not to trust him because he had a bad reputation but she didn't believe my father—and sure enough, with her money the man got the Argentine visas and disappeared.

Then the Dominican consul gave us two families a visa and we gratefully accepted it. My brother and I immediately read the Dominican newspaper "La Opinion" that the consul had given to my father. When I saw that there were movies and buses and taxis, I was very glad. I thought there would only be natives and people living in huts—like in the book "Monika Goes to Madagascar," a children's book, which I had read in Germany. Then we children pored over an old world map to find this island. Well, we couldn't. Now we were most concerned. My parents had found a lovely woman to teach us some Spanish while in London. She told us that we must look for Haiti in the Caribbean Sea, and that half of that island was Santo Domingo, or the Dominican Republic. In Haiti they spoke French while in the Dominican Republic they spoke Spanish.

After much back and forth and celebrating our departure at Auntie Heddy's home, we were ready to go by train to Glasgow on Oct. 2, 1939. Suddenly the phone rang. It was the steamship company informing us that the steamer could not leave because no convoy was available to accompany a commercial ship and we had to wait another week. That was a difficult week for us. On the 8th, at 8 p.m. the two families stood in the station taking leave of our English relatives. In the morning in Glasgow, we had something to eat, then went down to the docks where hundreds of people were waiting to get on the steamer.

All our trunks were opened and inspected. Finally, early evening we were allowed to board the "SS Cameronia." Off we finally sailed, accompanied by a convoy that continually searched the waters for German submarines. Many people were seasick, but I wasn't. As soon as it became dark, we had "blackout." We were not allowed to open port holes and turn on lights only when shades were drawn. No smoking on deck! We were lucky. We were not attacked but a number of transatlantic ships were.

On October 17, 1939 we saw the Statue of Liberty for the first time. Many cried. Despite my uncle and aunt's Canadian cousin waiting at the dock with permission to house us in her temporary New York City apartment, we were rushed off to Ellis Island. At that time, many refugees who had a transit visa would disappear in greater New York and the American authorities took extreme measures to prevent this.

So, there we were on Ellis Island—for 5 days. Our first glimpse of the United States and New York City through the bars on the windows of our jail!

Ellis Island, USA

What kind of island is that, and so near to New York City? We soon learned that this island is where, for many years, most immigrants were interned for several days—sometimes much longer—to be examined physically and questioned about their purpose for coming to the U.S.A. If the potential immigrant was sick, had no money, or had no one to sponsor him, he was often returned to the country he had just left. We had never heard about this island, and were totally, unpleasantly surprised. This was jail! Fences and cement walls surrounded us

Our days were spent in a huge hall. At one end were people from Europe, as I remember, and at the other end people from Asia and other exotic countries. I saw black Africans, white seamen with long beards from Turkey, turbaned people from all over Asia. While it was rather fascinating to me, it also was a bit frightening. I was not allowed to cross the hall and look or mingle with "those" people. Don't know if that was my parents' decree or the guards.

Wherever we went, to the toilet, the washroom, or the eating hall, there was a guard with a watch and a clicker in his hand, clicking every time somebody passed him. I still hear this clicker and I wonder now why we were counted everywhere we went. There wasn't much to go to. For the first two days, we didn't even get outside. We could barely see Manhattan through the high windows. We were prisoners.

Then the third day we were told that because some groups had raised their voices about these immigrants not being allowed to get any fresh air, we could now walk, in small groups, in the patio for half an hour, twice a day, at an appointed time. Again, as we passed through the door—click, click. And when we returned—click, click. But we were glad to have some fresh air and stretch our legs.

There was little to do except meet people, eat and sleep. The food wasn't good. Someone suggested to my parents to ask for kosher food, that it was better prepared, and so we did. We never kept a kosher household. This was my first experience. I found out that the food had hardly any salt or spices. And was hardly any better.

My parents didn't make friends easily but we children did. I remember playing chess with a young man from Greece. I spoke no Greek; he spoke 3 English words, "one, two, three." Chess was perfect except that I never played it before—but he was patient. My brother fell in love with a nice French girl and wasn't to be separated from her! Bedtime was at 9 p.m., and lights out at 10 p.m. Men and women were separated, so I slept with Mutti and another woman and her daughter in a small room with two bunk beds.

Time moved so slowly—at last, 5 days later, we were shipped back to a pier in Manhattan and boarded the "SS Coamo", one of the two Dominican ships that traveled between NYC and Ciudad Trujillo, the capital of Santo Domingo. What was awaiting us? What would be our future?

Life in Santo Domingo (the Dominican Republic) 1939-1946

October 25, 1939—we arrive in our new country! To my delight, I see big buildings, a fortress, and an active harbor. It's quite warm, the sun is shining, and people are on the pier looking expectantly up to our ship.

We are all nervous. As we get ready with our hand luggage, two Customs Officials are carefully examining our passports and entry papers. They gesture to indicate we are denied entry and cannot walk down the gangplank. My parents cannot believe this is happening. It turns out that I have become 14 years old since leaving England which makes me, they say, "an adult" and therefore we have to shell out more money. We manage to contact Aunt Heddy in London who promises to send the necessary additional money. With that promise, we are allowed to leave the ship and finally stand on Dominican soil! We are all utterly exhausted.

A lovely tall woman approached us on the pier and took us under her wing. Frau (Mrs.) Berg, who was working with the Jewish Committee, I believe, was going to put us up in her boarding house and help us get acclimatized. She was just wonderful, calmed us down, took care of everything (including having our crates warehoused), talked to us about life in our new homeland and we gratefully stayed with her and loved her Viennese food! I was installed on the roof, four floors up, in my own room! I couldn't wait to get up there and look over the city and the river. However, I was not alone. Rather large beetles with shiny brown wings were in my room. They were the famous "cucarachas" (cockroaches). They were all over the roof, their favorite playground, as well as in my room. It took me a while not to admire them but to step on them and kill them.

We learned that a Jewish agency, the Joint Distribution Committee, had recently opened an office in the capital. This agency was helping Jewish refugees all over the world, with the aid of private gifts and contributions. The Joint (as we called them) kept us and many others alive.

Frau Berg was priceless with her advice and introduction to a land we knew nothing about. She helped us find a house to rent, the first priority. A house! All my short life I was used to living in an apartment, and in a large city like Berlin. We moved into that house within a few weeks. Altogether we moved three times, the longest stay was our last house, which I remember the best.

Our first house had room for boarders and The Joint made an arrangement with us to take in other refugees who were expected from Europe. This gave us a small income and would help the others. The house had a little garden in the back with one fruit tree and a little green spot in front. We wondered how we would live there. But it all worked out quite well, at least as I saw it. We had much to learn and, thanks to Frau Berg, who was always available to help, we gradually made the transition to this totally different lifestyle.

Here are just a few things:

— learn Spanish
— how to deal with the subtropical climate
— how to deal with the many vendors that came to the door
— how to shop
— how to keep the ice box cold with a block of ice
— how to prevent ants from crawling over the food
— how to deal with the mosquitoes
— what to eat and what not to eat
— to never drink water that hadn't been boiled
— to always disinfect raw fruit and vegetables in the chemical solution of potassium permanganate

In general, the Dominican people were very friendly and curious about these newcomers though there wasn't much social mixing. Most of the inhabitants were Catholics. Where we lived people eked out an existence but were not as poor as those coming from the countryside. Of course we had a language problem, and very little else in common. My parents enrolled me in a public school. I stayed exactly two weeks. When I complained I didn't understand a word, they just took me out, even though I wanted to stay. Mother felt that it was not a good idea for me to mingle with ". . . the poor natives . . . Who knows what disease they may carry?" I would have learned much more Spanish had I stayed. My parents were very prejudiced, which I didn't understand at that time.

Some historical background

Our new homeland, Santo Domingo, or the Dominican Republic, is part of an island between Cuba and Puerto Rico. It was divided in 1697 into two states: Haiti and Santo Domingo. But first, in 1492, Christopher Columbus set foot on the eastern coast of this island before reaching America. Spain sent settlers and the island remained under Spanish rule until 1697.

Earlier, France had become interested in this island and started colonizing the western part of it mainly with slaves from Africa. Both France and Spain abused the hospitable native Indians. Spain lost interest in the island and ceded the western part to France in 1697. The island became better known as Haiti where French was spoken. There was much violence between these two peoples who spoke different languages and came from different cultures. Finally in 1777, under the Treaty of Aranjuez, a clear demarcation of land between Haiti and Santo Domingo was drawn.

Still, bloodshed continued until 1801 when the Haitian General Toussaint L'Ouverture gained control over both Santo Domingo and Haiti and kicked out the French. Haiti then refused to give back the eastern part of the island to the Dominicans. More fighting. In 1844 the Dominicans got their land back and eleven years later declared their independence. However, the new republic didn't do well. Overthrow after overthrow of government followed and the country plunged into financial ruin. The USA intervened three times (in 1905, 1912, and 1914). Then in 1916 the USA took over for six years and established a fairly stable government.

Just when things began to improve, a terrible hurricane swept the country in 1930. It caused a great loss of life as well as millions of dollars. It also gave opportunity to General Leonidas Rafael Trujillo Molina to seize power and rule as a dictator. Despite his ruthlessness, the country did become more stable. However, much of the wealth ended up in his and his family's pockets. Though he inflicted many horrors on his population, he was the only president who opened this small country to us Jews. He also sold some land up north to one of the Jewish agencies and the Sosua Settlement was created in late 1939, under the auspices of the DORSA (Dominican Republic Settlement Association).

Some geography

Approximately 19,000 square miles, Santo Domingo has many little rivers and brooks and the main river, the Ozama, flows into the capital. These waters make the land fertile. From north to south the country is narrow; from east to west a mountain range cuts through it. The Dominicans were proud of this mountain range and insisted that there was some snow on the highest peak.

You could drive from the north coast to the south coast in eleven hours, if: . . . you didn't get a flat tire in the isolated mountains; your water was not exhausted; your old car did not break down; there were no earthquakes; it had not rained too much; there were no landslides.

Climate

Santo Domingo is a beautiful country. It has a variety of magnificent flowers, tropical plants, palm trees and coconut trees—colorful but not so green because of the hot sun. It has some lovely beaches but also sharks in rocky waters.

The heat was almost unbearable for us during the first year. Eventually we became accustomed to temperatures ranging from 85 degrees F to 115 degrees F. I had to change my clothes five times a day. When I rode home on my bicycle at lunchtime, I would fall flat on my bed for several minutes to regain my strength. Between noon and 2 p.m. hardly a person was seen on the street. It was siesta time. At 2 p.m. people crept back to their work in the shade of houses or trees.

The difference between summer and winter became noticeable to us only after a few years. The nights and early mornings were cooler in the winter but the noon sun was just as scorching as in the summer. The rainy season started in January and lasted for almost six weeks. Rain came down in torrents. Within minutes the streets were inundated and nobody dared to leave home. Few people went to work. The poor, who mostly lived in wooden houses, built on the ground without a foundation, had to flee from the floods. The whole country became paralyzed. It was even too dangerous to travel as many rivers overflowed their low banks. Bridges were torn away and landslides occurred. Yet, these rains were the source of life to Dominican agriculture and nature. The torrential rains however did not bring relief from the heat and encouraged mosquitoes to breed and multiply in the stagnant waters and swamps. In Europe we had never experienced such huge downpours.

In September and October, the Dominicans feared another hurricane like the one that destroyed so much land in 1930. During these two months strong winds and breezes swept over the land. Whenever the possibility of a hurricane was announced, everybody went to church, bolted his doors and windows, took his children to a neighbor living in a stone building, buried what he treasured in a safe place, and despaired. Many women ran into the streets, wringing their hands, crying and shouting: "misecordia, misecordia," and making everybody more nervous. Occasionally earth tremors and even small earthquakes occurred. I slept peacefully through all of them.

The Capital

Ciudad Trujillo, now called Santo Domingo, (changed after Generalísimo Trujillo was killed in 1961) is situated on the south coast. In 1939 it had a population of about 110,000. Everybody knew everybody else. When a stranger came to town, a whisper would begin: "¿Quién es (Who is he?)"; "¿De dónde viene (Where does he come from?) "; "¿Dónde vive? (Where does he live?)"; "¿Es un Yankee? (Is he a Yankee?)". Strangers were very welcome. They seldom haggled, paid good prices and made excellent topics for gossip.

La Capital, as the city is usually called, had two main avenues, one with more expensive stores and the other the cheaper shopping area. Along the oceanfront there is a lovely avenue lined with tall palm trees swaying in the wind. I remember an expensive hotel there and beautiful mansions. It was always a treat to walk along this street under the trees, watch the Caribbean Sea waves swell up and hit against the rocks. You couldn't go swimming there because the water was deep and sharks were often present.

When I walked in the city, young loafers would linger at the street corners and eye every girl up and down and make suggestive remarks. I wasn't used to this and tried to evade these shocking and mocking eyes. I was so embarrassed to hear "You are beautiful"; "You have lovely legs"; "You have a pinching behind"; and "You are ripe for marriage." These men were everywhere, even in the main park of the city where everybody, especially the young people, walked in the evening around and around the kiosk to listen to the band playing there, to make friends, to flirt and to be admired by the men. It was the highlight of entertainment.

Our Jewish Group

I estimate that we were 60 families with children, mainly from Austria, Germany, and a few from Czechoslovakia and Poland. We soon formed a youth group of about 20 boys and girls between 15 and 21 years old. We often went on short trips to explore the surrounding areas, or just gathered somewhere to be together. Dr. Robitchek, a scholarly man who had many art books, volunteered to give us art history lessons twice a week. I loved it! It was my introduction to this exciting world.

I also went to the American University run by a Dr. Morgan. I decided one day to just walk into the school to see what would happen. Surprisingly, nothing happened. Nobody noticed me. I simply sat down in the back of his class and listened to his lectures on English/American literature. By then I understood enough English to follow his lectures. Afterwards, I would try to find the book he'd lectured on and read it. One was *The Legend of Sleepy Hollow*. Determined to improve my English, I took four pages and looked up every unknown word in my dictionary. I ended up learning about 30 words from every page.

Our youth group helped us all to adjust better than our parents. We also were young and enjoyed ourselves. We even presented a play by Arthur Schnitzler and invited our parents to the grand opening. I had the "demanding" role of Cora, who was hypnotized and had to pretend to sleep throughout that scene, never uttering a word! Later, some of us dared to go to the U.S.O. (United Service Organization), a social club for the American Coast Guard boys. The U.S. Coastguard was stationed in Ciudad Trujillo in 1942 because of rumors that German U-boats had been sighted up north. Everybody wanted to meet American boys. One of our girls brought her Dominican boyfriend into our group. They eventually married. I had a Dominican girl friend but she never joined our group.

I don't really know how the other Jewish families survived. Some did find work or opened a small store, but it was difficult. Many of us were supported by The Joint. Even though we rented out two rooms, it was a meager income. My parents sold some of the things they had brought with them. The Oriental rugs went quickly as did our Rosenthal set of dishes (miraculously mostly intact), and some of our paintings. Somehow we acquired more books and opened a lending library. I was in charge of this library. I read every one of the books, some in German and some in English. The first book I read was *Rebecca* by Daphne Du Maurier and to this day I remember the opening lines "Last night I dreamed I went to Manderley again." It was a wonderful book that I recommended to all our readers!

I was the first one in our family to earn some money. A wealthy Jewish family, also immigrants from Germany, needed a babysitter for their 4-year old daughter. I accepted and took care of her for a few weeks. At age 14, I knew it all including how to take care of little children and how parents did it all wrong! So, when she sucked her thumb so often, I knew exactly what to do: put mustard on her finger. I didn't last long in that job.

My parents learned of a Scotsman who ran an import/ export business and employed refugees. He didn't pay well but he provided work. It was so terrible for the young and also older men not to do anything and not be able to provide for their families. It certainly affected my father. But Mr. Lockie only employed young people. So one day father took me to him. I was a bit nervous. I had heard he had a terrible temper. He was an imposing older man, white-haired and stout. He said that he wouldn't employ my father but perhaps me. Did I do any stenography? I had learned steno but only in German. Mr. Lockie then proposed that I go to a "commercial school." My father said we had no money. Mr. Lockie offered to pay $5.00 (Dominican dollars) per month for my school and that I should come back to him in 3 months so he could see my progress. Thus I ended up in a Spanish business school learning English stenography. It took me more than 3 months to learn it but Mr. Lockie finally employed me as a typist. I was the first one in my family to earn a wage! I was so proud.

I loved going to work. The office was right on the waterfront and I had a wonderful view of what was going on there. I managed to acquire a bicycle and enjoyed riding along the main street El Conde down to the waterfront twice a day. At work I met my first Dominican friend, Olga, a young girl my age. She showed me how to type invoices, which we did most of the time. As we became friends, we competed to see who was faster and typed furiously in competition.

We became really good friends. She also had a bicycle and we often biked together. She was very good for me. She helped me through a very difficult time with my parents. They were not adjusting well and there was much friction at home. Olga was a Roman Catholic and very friendly with some nuns. Eventually she became a nun.

We had a rabbi, actually two rabbis. One was of the Conservative faith from Germany, and the other of Orthodox faith from Poland. So we did have services and I became religious for a while. One of our boarders took me on Fridays to the Conservative service. I liked it very much and also the singing at times. When he left, I didn't go anymore because there was friction between the two rabbis. With only one room, the service was divided between those two. I felt very uncomfortable with that situation.

Whenever we heard a ship was arriving from Europe, many of us rushed down to the pier to see if an acquaintance or possibly a family member was on it. We would also help if necessary. One day, when my father went again to watch refugees coming off the ship, he saw a young woman with a baby in her arms and her tall husband. They seemed vaguely familiar to him. He checked with Frau Berg, who had lists of the passengers, and discovered the young people were related to him through a cousin in Vienna.

Naturally, they moved in with us and I happily discovered that we had Austrian relatives. Mutti was delighted to have them stay with us because of the baby. The husband soon left for Brazil where he hoped to make a good living. The young woman's mother (Father's cousin) had fled to the U.S.A. and lived in New York City. She applied for a visa for me to come to the States when I nervously contacted her in 1943. It took several years before I was granted an entry visa.

Daily Living Within the Capital

The so-called middle income group lived in the city. Most houses were dark, hot and not well furnished but had at least electricity and running water. The living quarters of the low-income group were outside the city and in much poorer condition. Their small wooden houses had only one or two sparsely furnished rooms lacking such comforts as electricity, gas, running water or a radio. Most used kerosene lamps or candles for light. Many did not have sleeping or cooking facilities. They had a small portable iron stove, heated by coal, upon which they put a pan to broil bacalao (their fish) or boil rice and beans.

How different was the residential section of the wealthy and of foreigners! Wide streets were lined with palm trees under whose shade one could seek relief from the burning sun. Each home had one or two garages, a garden facing the street and another larger one in the back, and a porch surrounding the house, with a splendid variety of flowers and plants in every front garden. The lovely and tasteful architecture delighted me when I rode through the streets with my bicycle.

The further out I went, the more I became aware of the foreign atmosphere—the American colony. The American architecture was so different from the Old Spanish homes. Most American homes had mosquito screens and all other modern comforts, such as an electric stove, an electric iron, tiled bathrooms, hot and cold running water, and a clean modern kitchen with a refrigerator.

These comforts I ardently wished for us. A refrigerator was out of question for us. We had a wooden ice cooler and had to learn how to keep the ice cold. You wrap newspapers around the ice clump you just bought and hope that the paper keeps the ice from melting before the next day.

An electric stove—what luxury! My father had to get up every morning one hour before breakfast to start the fire burning with a match on the charcoal in our brick stove and put on the water to boil. If the coal was damp, it did not burn. Then the whole family had to get up, stand in the kitchen blowing on the coals until they caught fire and filled the kitchen with smoke. We would stand there, coughing, with tears streaking down our blackened cheeks.

When I ironed, I had to put two heavy old-fashioned irons on the hot stove and use them alternately. I thought I would never see the day when I would iron with an electric iron.

Somebody gave us an old radio that sometimes even worked. When it did, we were able to hear news from the U.S. Usually we had to rely on friends to tell us what was happening in the world.

Shopping

The more reliable stores were on main street El Conde. These stores were fairly clean and more honest. The other street, Avenida Mella, was a dirty street, with many little shops. The owners were of questionable character and gave you a price of an article before you asked and lowered it before you started to bargain. Only those who knew how to bargain went there. I once bought three yards of material to sew a skirt at such a good price that I felt suspicious. At home I found that

I had been cheated of a quarter yard. It took some time to learn the art of haggling. How I hated it, in the beginning!

Later I became a master at it. I had bought a bicycle second hand for $17 and decided to sell it after using it for three years. It looked like new because I took good care of it. My first customer was a 15-year-old native boy who came on a Sunday morning at seven o'clock. He looked my bicycle over, while I was standing next to him in my pajamas with sleep in my eyes. He turned and said "$25." I did not even look at him; I shoved him towards the door and said "adiós." He quickly offered $30. I didn't say anything. He offered $40, I merely looked at him. He offered $45, I showed some interest. He finally came up to $50. Then I said: "You get it for $53 cash." He took out his purse, put the money on the table and rode off. A good deal, for me!

Instead of department stores, we had to get used to buy each article at specific stores such as tools only in a hardware store, toilet articles only at pharmacies. These shops were very small. Only one store had two floors and a larger variety of articles. Most Dominicans sewed their own clothes, so a big variety of cloth materials was available. Generally there was a very high duty on these materials but importing them was a very good business, if you knew the customs officials.

At every corner you could find a pharmacy. They made money by giving so-called injections. Many ignorant natives went to the pharmacist if they had a headache or a stomachache, or a more serious complaint, and the pharmacist took "good care" of them.

Although there was a market in the city, it was so much easier to buy food and other essentials at your house. The first one to come was the milkman, who at five o'clock in the morning, ringing a little bell, filled the pots on the porch with milk well mixed with water; and you prayed he put them back in the shade and that nobody stole them. During the entire morning you could hear the merchants cry their praises of the wares they sold. In torn clothes they came, both men and women, their feet touching the ground as they rode little mules packed with sacks and baskets. You called them to your porch, and then the haggling was on. You bought green beans already cut and cleaned; you bought oranges, peeled if you so wished; you bought your best vegetable from the Chinese, and you learned not to buy too often from the same person.

Worst of the merchants was the coal man. You had him open a sack, and if you liked the coal, he brought it into your kitchen and dumped it into a box under the brick stove. Only then, when the bottom came to light, did you realize what junk you had bought. Half the sack was full of small pieces and blackened stones which didn't burn.

Most important was the iceman. Unreliable, he could make your hair turn white, particularly if you had a boarding house. Few houses had refrigerators. We paid 15 cents every day for ice that should last at least until the early evening in our decrepit icebox. He cheerfully assured us he would bring ice "mañana" at the same time. But did he? Without ice, the milk turned sour, the butter melted, all the "cucarachas" hiding in the icebox would run over the food. There were no cold drinks, only angry voices.

The Waterfront

Under President Trujillo, often called "El Jefe", the dirty, shallow waterfront that prevented larger steamers from docking became a beautiful harbor. The mouth of the Ozama River was dredged, the pier paved with asphalt, warehouses enlarged, offices, and a Customs House were erected.

The two years I worked for Mr. Lockie there, I could watch from the window of my desk the loading of rice, cacao, sugar, coffee, fruits, chickens and coconuts. The loading of live cattle was especially interesting. The cattle came mostly from President Trujillo's estates and were well fed. Between 5,000 and 6,000 heads were exported yearly to neighboring islands: Puerto Rico,

Martinique, Guadeloupe, Curacao and Trinidad. A few men, keeping the cattle together with slings and much shouting, would drive some hundred heads through the streets. Often an animal would become panicky before being hoisted on board and would kick and fight for its freedom, unsuccessfully.

Many products were also imported. Watching the unloading of flour, farina, ketchup, mustard, potatoes, fish, tires, cars, trucks, bicycles, and many other items was also fun. The unloading of cement was particularly unpleasant because we then had to close all the windows in our office and run around with handkerchiefs covering our mouths. During the rainy season, the unloading of flour and cement was a problem. When the first drops fell, the longshoremen ran faster than ever before to cover the unloaded merchandise with large canvases, praying that everything under it would remain dry. I remember one time when a Canadian ship bringing cement could not unload for seven days because of the rain.

Drunken sailors were no novelty. The police were called, and after a few blows on the head, the sailor was removed in an ambulance.

When a freighter came in, two or three women would appear around noon, sit in the shade and prepare food for the workers over a tiny charcoal stove. Most of the dock workers would try to get their food on credit by embracing the women, whispering pretty words into their ears, making jokes and slapping their fannies until they had conquered. On payday the fight was on. Huge arguments started, with the women shouting and cursing, while the men roared with laughter. Finally the overseer would settle the dispute. On Monday, it began all over again.

Little boys earned a few cents by passing water to the longshoremen on duty, or cleaning boots of officers, or selling candy.

Between noon and 2:00 p.m. work stopped, and the men lay down in the shade. Some of them played dice, others sang, some slept. And we in the office went home.

During the war, the American Coast Guard made the wharf really popular. School children, young girls and women would pass by and stare at the neat small boats, talk to the sailors in broken English, and enjoy themselves.

Even when there were no boats, something surely would always happen.

Daily Occurrences

The poverty of the natives was great, and stealing was common. A servant girl (called "muchacha") received only $5 or $6 (Dominican dollars) per month plus meals and often bad treatment. An English-speaking girl usually made twice as much and consequently was very proud. How often did we find some of our silverware in our muchacha's pocket as she went home, or saw one of the merchants peeling beans in front of our eyes with one of our knives! Our sheets and towels disappeared rapidly. We tried to raise chickens. Our neighbor took three and had a good supper; a man on the street sold one back to my mother; the others we never found.

A man entered the house and stole the dollar bills lying on a table next to my sleeping parents. Another slipped into the front room one afternoon and stole my father's fountain pen while he was dozing on the porch. In the evening, mounted policemen rode through the streets in search of thieves. Yet, to steal was not as serious an offense as it is in the U.S.A. I cannot see what other resource remained to abused natives who were so poor that often they did not have shoes to wear or another meal to eat than just rice with beans and mangoes. There was a mango tree near our house. Often small boys would come and pick up mangos that had fallen down. Many of these youngsters had distended stomachs from eating only this fruit for want of other food.

Many young boys also earned a few cents by selling peanuts. "A handful for the pretty lady!" With a big smile on their dirty faces, swinging a can with a little fire burning beneath, they would pour a handful of hot peanuts into the cup of your hand for a penny. Others cleaned shoes. Every Sunday morning a couple of little urchins knocked at our door and laden with many shoes they would look for shade under a tree and sing while they worked for hours polishing a pair. Some tried their luck by selling one tenth of a ticket of the National Lottery. The boys ran from house to house, inducing you to buy; you were sure to win when you bought one twenty-four hours before the Sunday drawing. The first prize was $15,000 (Dominican dollars). My brother won $2 twice in four years. The owner of the National Lottery was one of the richest men in Santo Domingo.

There is much rhythm and music in Latin American countries, and Santo Domingo is no exception. The laborers, who ripped up the streets to lay new asphalt, would stand in a row, alternate in lifting their hoes and with rhythmic cries would accompany each stroke, up and down. With a whistle the postman, on a bicycle, threw the mail on the porch. A low-toned bell announced the man in white, who, balancing a large box on his head, sold sweets and candies for 1 and 5 cents. The high tones of a flute drew the children out of the houses to run toward the ice-cream man who, in the evenings, pushed his little cart through the streets. The blaring radios in the neighboring stores made less agreeable sounds. All morning long on Sundays, they would announce the winning lottery tickets.

Mosquitoes

You could never get used to them and their humming while buzzing around your head when you were relaxing in the rocking chair on the porch, particularly in the evening. Around and around your head they would fly, and you would try to catch them by clapping your hands together over your head, to no avail. They would only attack your bare legs.

To sleep you had to be under a mosquito net. There were two kinds of nets, the square ones and the cone-like ones. The advantage of the square ones, which attached to four posts on the bed, is that you could catch a mosquito. With the cone-shaped net, which falls from the ceiling, they fly to the highest point and you can't reach them. Without this net, you get bitten all over making sleep impossible. The fight with mosquitoes when we were there was a constant. We learned to use the green menthol coils. You light the coil with a match and the smell and smoke chased the mosquitoes away for a while. Some people get bitten much more than others. I have an olive skin but those little beasts prefer light-skinned flesh, so I was not bitten so terribly.

Our Boarding House

In our first house, we had a lovely family—parents with two daughters—from Worms, Germany. They arrived during the rainy season and got thoroughly wet when they had to walk not even a minute from the taxi to the entrance of our house. They were just dripping with water. It was not a good reception after all the strain of coming to a strange land all the way from France where they were interned in Gurs, a detention camp in southern France. They were an interesting family and we soon became great friends. A few months later they moved up north to the Jewish Sosua Settlement.

In our third house we had enough room to rent out 3 rooms because my brother also moved up north to the Sosua Settlement. For a while we had only European refugees. Then a beautiful young Dominican woman came who stayed with us several months. She was a poetess and I was much intrigued by her. She did have a "sugar daddy," one of Trujillo's friends I assume, who picked her up weekly in a black limousine. I was very innocent in those days. One of my girl friends then told me about the "birds and the bees."

Later we rented a room to three young refugee fellows, two from Vienna, one from Frankfurt. I enjoyed them very much. They tried to make a living in woodworking by fashioning wooden trinkets in a little shop they opened. They worked very hard and usually came home very tired and very dirty. One day they brought home a little gray-black dog and gave her to my mother. Mother decided to bathe that little dog only to discover she was white! Mother was very happy to have a dog and took her wherever she went. One day she took her to the movies. When Mother came walking back, a man tried to embrace her. She cried out to her dog . . . and the dog ran off! Nothing happened to Mother, though.

A young girl who decided to leave Sosua and find work in the city moved in. She fell in love with one of our three fellows and they carried on a hot relationship. One day Father looked out of a window and saw the pathway along our house full of condoms! He was furious!

Later on we had some sailors from the American Coast Guard staying with us. It was good for us, financially. By then I knew plenty of English. I enjoyed these boys. One was from Arkansas ready to marry me. The other was a seasoned flirt from Chicago. Another was mad about baseball. My mother enjoyed a more serious American who was "colored." He was very nice and thoughtful and explained to my mother the prejudice and difficulties of the Black Americans in North America. We were only vaguely aware of this. By then my father had a sudden heart attack and died in April 1944, so it was good for my mother to have this sympathetic friend.

Sosua

This Jewish settlement was a gift by El Jefe, General Trujillo, to Jewish refugees. He sold the land rather cheaply to the Jewish agency that formed the DORSA. In the original plan it was meant to be populated by perhaps 10,000 Jewish refugees. It was land around a beautiful bay, near the city of Puerto Plata on the north coast. The first group arrived, I think, in the beginning of 1940. This group of young men and women was called "the Trainees" and came from England where they had found refuge. The next group came from Switzerland, and then families started to arrive. I suppose it was the DORSA who sent investigators to Europe to find young boys and girls who had nowhere to go and thus were offered a new life.

The first groups had to live in bare barracks hastily built, had community cooking, and everybody had to pitch in with housework and kitchen duties. Later, curtains were installed, finally barracks were built just for couples. Still later, houses were built on stilts and farmland was given to families to try to cultivate the land. Various shops sprang up: mattresses were built, a woodworking shop, a dairy, a cheese maker, a shoemaker, a sausage maker, and others. People who had various skills were given the opportunity to develop them there. There was a hospital and babies were born. My first friend, who was our first boarder, became a baby nurse. A rabbi arrived and Jewish service started. Most of these young Jewish immigrants had never been on a farm. Some learned a bit about agriculture on the Hachsharahs (small Jewish youth camps originally preparing young Zionist groups for immigrating to Palestine) that had sprung up in the late 1920s around Berlin with the help of Jewish agencies to train young people to make a living, mainly as farmers.

I loved to go up there and visit my brother. This was possible for me when the "camion" (truck) came down to the city to pick up people or equipment. The first time I went, I helped peel potatoes and vegetables. Everybody had to chip in and hardly any Dominican was employed. Later, when the tomatoes were rotting and vegetables became riddled with worms, and other calamities befell the new "farmers," then local help was hired who knew exactly what to do. They used drums to scare off unwanted vermin.

Up there, I also had a lot of fun. There were always dances and so many young people. Our group in the Capital was very small. My brother tried to make me ride a mule. I reluctantly got on but the mule didn't budge. I kicked it with my heel, but it still wouldn't move. Finally my brother got on it and the mule immediately trotted away.

Everybody was very busy. Suddenly I remembered the Elephant Baby, the girl who had been with me in the London hostel in August and who didn't meet her mother in Belgium because the war broke out. Didn't she tell me that her father was in the Dominican Republic? Sure enough, I found him and his wife in Sosua. They were hoping that their daughter would come soon.

Many stories can be told about Sosua. This close living prompted many happy and unhappy relationships. Altogether there were about 800 people up there. It still exists but only with a few people who are working in the dairy and perhaps the sausage factory. I have lost touch with them.

Other Things

After I worked for maybe two years at Mr. Lockie's firm, I saw an ad in the newspaper asking for English-speaking secretaries. I applied and got a great job with a bank set up by the U.S. Agriculture Department that was dealing with loans and mortgages. I was paid a pretty good salary and was very proud of being the only money-earning family member. The job was far over my head, and the bank soon hired the fastest typist I have ever seen. They didn't fire me. Instead they gave me things to translate. I even became an "expert" on the mosquito and its behavior.

After the sudden death of my father in 1944, I received the American visa from my newly found aunt in New York two years later and I left Santo Domingo in June 1946, by plane to Miami, then by bus to New York City, where I still live. Mother followed me at the end of 1947.

Lisa's
Photo
Album

Berlin
1930s

The Dominican Republic
1940s

#1—Berlin—1926.
Mutti and Vati
at the race track.

#2—Berlin—1928.
My brother Hans-
Wolfgang takes
little me for a walk
in "Tiergarten" park.

#3—Berlin—1936.
Mutti with my brother Hans-Wolfgang.

#4—Mutti and I in Berlin—1937.

#5—Berlin—1937. I win the 50-meter race for my Jewish school, the Adass Jisroel Lyceum.

Deutsches Reich

J

Kennkarte

A 102 (19.3») ✪

Kennort:	*Berlin*
Kennnummer:	*A 066 948*
Gültig bis	*21. März* 19*44*
Name	*Klein*
Vornamen	*Lisa-Sara*
Geburtstag	*1. Oktober 1925*
Geburtsort	*Berlin*
Beruf	*ohne*
Unveränderliche Kennzeichen	*fehlen*
Veränderliche Kennzeichen	*fehlen*
Bemerkungen:	*Keine.*

Rechter Zeigefinger

Linker Zeigefinger

Lisa Sara Klein
(Unterschrift des Kennkarteninhabers)

Berlin, den *21. März* 19*39*

Der Polizeipräsident in Berlin

(Unterschrift des ausfertigenden Beamten)

#6—Berlin, March 21, 1939. The infamous Jewish Identification Card every Jew had to carry, showing the left ear and 2 finger prints, date of birth and other details, including the addition of the name "Sara" to a woman's first name, and the name "Israel" to a man's first name.

#7—The Dominican Republic—1941—Ciudad Trujillo. Mutti on the verandah of our last house.

#8—The Dominican Republic—1942—Ciudad Trujillo. Lisa standing in front of the verandah with Vati sitting in the background.

#9—The Dominican Republic—1941—Sosua. Landscape up north with Jewish settler and 2 Dominicans bringing cows to the dairy.

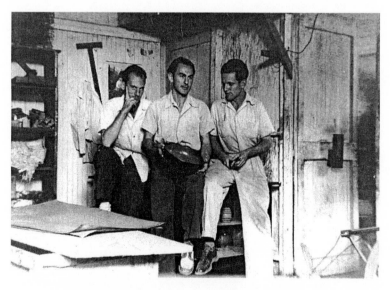

#10—The Dom. Republic—1943—Ciudad Trujillo. Our three young Jewish boarders from Sosua in their tiny workshop.

Epilogue

Of the four of us, Ellen Stein is the one who had the vision to have us remember our childhood in Berlin, and thus our stories emerged. Ellen has known two of us for a long time. She and I met again only recently. In Year 2000 each of us finally accepted an invitation by the Mayor of Berlin to visit our old hometown, all expenses paid. Ellen recognized my name on the list of invitees and remembered me from our school, the "Adass Jisroel." And so we met again on the plane to Berlin after 62 years! She is a dynamo and an inspiration to us three.

Writing my story was not an easy task but, with Ellen's encouragement, I am glad I did. I do not remember much of my childhood in Berlin, only bits and pieces of the many unpleasant and frightening events in the 1930s. As I wrote about what I remembered, I came to the conclusion that whoever reads our stories would want to know what happened to us later. So I decided on giving a glimpse into the seven years of living in the Dominican Republic. I may have some facts wrong and apologize herewith for unintentional mistakes particularly in my Dominican Republic recollections.

Not much is written about this island that at a certain time was the only country that accepted Jewish refugees. (It also accepted refugees from Spain, the "Loyalists", who fled from General Franco's Fascist government in 1937 or thereabouts.) The difficulty of facing the unknown and the challenge of this complete change of life was overpowering for my parents, particularly my father. He was too hurt, too disappointed and too unbending to have the patience and willingness to deal with this different and poorer life. Both he and my mother had a tough time of it.

To us, the younger generation, it was a challenge to fit in, to understand, to learn the different customs of living and to respect them. It certainly widened my horizon and my curiosity about the many different cultures, different religions and different mores in this wide world. I am glad to have had this experience and will always feel a great warmth and appreciation toward the Dominican Republic and its people, a small country that opened its arms to us strangers.

Despite the killing of millions of my Jewish brethren by Nazi Germany, those of us who survived are scattered all over the world, more than ever before, in Latin America, North America, Australia, eastern Asia and other regions. We bring culture, the arts and deep-seated social concerns to wherever we immigrate. We also are a varied group with different religious points of view but wherever we settle we enrich that country. Perhaps this is why we are called "The Wandering Jews" and perhaps that is why this happens to us every now and then in the history of Planet Earth.

Lisa Klein . New York City . 2005

Millar Guthrie

EDITOR

Comments from our Editor

Ellen and I met after my college classmate Kenneth Stein displayed the good sense to marry her. We continued our friendship even after she was widowed. When Ellen returned from a trip to Berlin in the year 2000, she decided to write about her childhood memories, asking me if I, as a retired editor, would proofread and edit what she wrote. I agreed, and Ellen invited three of her friends to join us in this venture.

The result has been an interesting journey for me. I met, via computer, her school friends: Daisy, Marcelle and Lisa, who became her co-authors. They each entrusted me with intimate details of their experiences as Jewish girls living in 1930s Berlin.

Dredging up these memories brought back feelings that were difficult for them to write about. Reading their experiences was a revelation to me because, while they were being scorned for their religion, during the same years, I spent playing, riding my bike with friends as well as trying to pass, with minimal studying, my school subjects. Such different childhood memories!

The four co-authors and I had numerous editorial differences, even a few stormy arguments via the Internet and occasionally over the phone. I believe the writers are satisfied with the outcome. I was impressed with the fluency in English they displayed as they submitted their text for review. They each learned English after escaping Germany.

I admire these four women for having been able, not only to survive, but to build happy and successful lives after such difficult beginnings. All in all, it has been a fascinating and very informative couple of years for me and, indeed, for all five of us.

Millar Guthrie . North Carolina . 2005